Unlikely
Utopia

Also by Michael Adams

Sex in the Snow
The Surprising Revolution in Canadian Social Values

Better Happy Than Rich?
Canadians, Money and the Meaning of Life

Fire and Ice
The United States, Canada, and the Myth of Converging Values

American Backlash
The Untold Story of Social Change in the United States

Unlikely Utopia

THE SURPRISING
TRIUMPH OF **CANADIAN PLURALISM**

MICHAEL ADAMS
WITH AMY LANGSTAFF

VIKING
CANADA

VIKING CANADA

Published by the Penguin Group

Penguin Group (Canada), 90 Eglinton Avenue East, Suite 700, Toronto, Ontario, Canada
M4P 2Y3 (a division of Pearson Canada Inc.)

Penguin Group (USA) Inc., 375 Hudson Street, New York, New York 10014, U.S.A.
Penguin Books Ltd, 80 Strand, London WC2R 0RL, England
Penguin Ireland, 25 St Stephen's Green, Dublin 2, Ireland (a division of Penguin Books Ltd)
Penguin Group (Australia), 250 Camberwell Road, Camberwell, Victoria 3124, Australia
(a division of Pearson Australia Group Pty Ltd)
Penguin Books India Pvt Ltd, 11 Community Centre, Panchsheel Park, New Delhi – 110 017,
India
Penguin Group (NZ), 67 Apollo Drive, Rosedale, North Shore 0632, New Zealand
(a division of Pearson New Zealand Ltd)
Penguin Books (South Africa) (Pty) Ltd, 24 Sturdee Avenue, Rosebank, Johannesburg 2196,
South Africa

Penguin Books Ltd, Registered Offices: 80 Strand, London WC2R 0RL, England

First published 2007

1 2 3 4 5 6 7 8 9 10   (RRD)

Copyright © Michael Adams, 2007

Author representation: Westwood Creative Artists
94 Harbord Street, Toronto, Ontario M5S 1G6

Dialogue from *Little Mosque on the Prairie* used with permission of WestWind Pictures.

Manufactured in the U.S.A.

Library and Archives Canada Cataloguing in Publication data available upon request.

ISBN-13: 978-0-670-06368-0
ISBN-10: 0-670-06368-1

Visit the Penguin Group (Canada) website at **www.penguin.ca**

Special and corporate bulk purchase rates available; please see
www.penguin.ca/corporatesales or call 1-800-810-3104, ext. 477 or 474

For Ranbir Singh, Ashley Naipaul,
and Françoise Yessaya Keddy

Contents

Introduction
The Good News and the Bad News

Celebrate progress. Don't wait to get perfect.

—Ann McGee-Cooper

THIS BOOK is a good-news story about Canadian multiculturalism. It argues that immigration and the social diversity that flows from it are working well in many respects—much better than one might expect from watching the evening news or reading the anxious predictions of many of our intellectuals. It also defends the claim that Canada is good at managing diversity, arguing that this claim is neither vacuous national boosterism nor a quaint, deluded idea lifted from some 1970s government brochure. There is ample empirical evidence to suggest that Canada *is* special, both in its social conditions and in the way its people (Canadians new and old) respond to those conditions.

This book does not claim that things are perfect. It does not argue that Canada is free of racism and discrimination, nor does it contest or ignore the fact that poverty is concentrated among non-white Canadians. It does not claim that employment outcomes for newcomers to this country are where they should be—indeed, these outcomes *must* improve if the positive trends I sketch in these pages are to continue.

Similarly, this book does not deny that Canadians (of many backgrounds) are experiencing some anxiety about current policies related to immigration and multiculturalism. Our own data suggest that Canadians are indeed starting to worry that this country may have bitten off more than it can chew when it comes to the integration of newcomers of vastly different religious, cultural, and ideological backgrounds. It is precisely that worry, and the more exaggerated version of it which claims that Canada is a powder keg of ethnic strife waiting to explode, that this book is meant to address.

In chapter one I describe Canadian public attitudes about immigration, multiculturalism, and ethnic and religious difference. When compared with a host of other countries' citizenry, Canadians emerge as exceptionally open to people of different backgrounds and exceptionally positive about the contributions newcomers make. Newcomers themselves also register high levels of pride in Canada and considerable optimism about their lot in this country: according to Statistics Canada, 84 percent of recent immigrants (after four years in the country) say that if they had it to do over again, they'd make the same decision and come to Canada.[1]

In chapter two I go beyond opinion surveys to look at some "facts on the ground" about how newcomers and their children are really faring in this society: the economic outcomes they're achieving, the neighbourhoods they're living in, their involvement in the political process, and who they're marrying. Although the picture is, of course, complicated, when we look at the data on how Canadians old and new are living and working together—particularly in this country's major cities— we have many reasons for optimism.

Chapter three looks at the attitudes of (and about) a group that has been much in the news in the past half-decade: Canadian Muslims. In the winter of 2006–07 my public-opinion research firm, Environics, conducted the first-ever survey of Muslims living in Canada. I think Canadians will be as fascinated and surprised as I was to see the attitudes and opinions of Muslims in this country, a group we often see represented in the news media (seldom in a positive light) but from which we rarely hear directly.

In chapter four I consider how issues of migration and pluralism are playing out in Quebec. I examine the unique concerns and discussions that characterize the distinct society's approach to newcomers, and the diversity these newcomers bring to a province that has traditionally been more homogeneous (both linguistically and religiously) than the rest of Canada.

With the exception of our survey of Canadian Muslims, this book does not present much data that are altogether unknown. I don't reveal shocking secrets about the Canadian psyche or announce mounds of earth-shattering new research. What this book does is take what we know—what we know from the national census and Statistics Canada; what we know from the empirical work of geographers and social scientists; what we know from public opinion polling (both by Environics and by other organizations)—and consider this knowledge from a perspective of moderate optimism rather than knee-jerk alarmism.

This does not in itself strike me as a very radical undertaking, but given current discussions of diversity and multiculturalism in this country, it seems to strike others as rather audacious. During my work on this book, whenever I told someone that I was writing about multiculturalism in Canada they'd nod soberly as if to say, "I know: bad." When I explain that I think there's in fact good reason to see the glass as half full, I'm generally met with puzzlement: But what about the riots (by largely minority youth) in the suburbs of Paris? they ask. What about the murder of Dutch filmmaker Theo van Gogh at the hands of a Muslim radical? What about the ethnic enclaves (or are they ghettos?) in Canadian cities? What about *homegrown terror*?

I can only wait until they reach the end of the list—invariably a sprawling, global one that sees the world as increasingly engulfed by racial, ethnic, and religious strife—and ask why they think the Paris riots, for example, count as the death knell of Canadian multiculturalism. "Well, if it can happen there ..." is usually the reply. Before we assume that what happens "there" will automatically happen here and send parliamentary committees on fact-finding missions to foreign lands, perhaps we'd better take a longer look at what's happening here right now. I believe that when we do we'll see some things that demand deep thinking and ongoing vigilance. But we'll also see plenty of good news, plenty of cause for optimism, and plenty of evidence that Canada is working remarkably well given the scale of the social changes we've set in motion. So well, in fact, that instead of cataloguing all the things going wrong in this country, we might be better off trying to figure out why things are going so well here relative to elsewhere; as far as I am aware, nobody knows for sure. Such self-examination is a good idea not because it will allow us to rest on our self-satisfied laurels, but because it will help us design wise policies and make smart investments to keep us on the right track.

Some of Canada's success with diversity can be chalked up to experience: we've always relied on immigration for population growth, and we were the first country to adopt an official policy of multiculturalism. Some of the country's success might be attributed to our immigration point system, which has ensured that the bulk of newcomers to Canada have arrived with a tremendous amount to contribute economically, socially, and culturally (contributions that we're not consistently, at the moment, finding ways to honour and reward appropriately). Some of it might be attributed to the history of Canada's "charter groups," the British and French, which have always had to accommodate and live with one another. They have done so peacefully, if sometimes resentfully and acrimoniously, since the battle on the Plains of Abraham. Finally, there's always the possibility that Canadians are just morally superior to everyone else, an opinion some of my critics assume I embrace, but frankly this seems like a long shot. Whatever the reasons, Canadians of diverse backgrounds do, by and large, appear to be living fairly successfully together, as this book will attempt to show.

But if this is true—and there is much research to suggest that it is—then why are we constantly telling ourselves (in our newspapers and at the dinner table) that things are going so badly?

For one thing, there's a bad-news story to suit every political persuasion. Some people are inclined to think that Canada has too much immigration and that once immigrants are installed here, they're not encouraged aggressively enough to "become Canadian" and adopt the secular, liberal, consumerist values of the majority. For these people, many of whom you'll find on the political "right," the idea that ethnic enclaves are springing up in Canadian cities, that newcomer and second-generation youth are ready to explode into violence, that an ever-growing population of people not only don't care to adapt to Canadian life but don't much like Canada at all … well, it all makes perfect sense. They never thought multiculturalism was a good idea to begin with, so the fact that it's turning out to be a disaster is, if regrettable, satisfyingly predictable.

Others, generally on the political "left," are happy with immigration and multiculturalism but believe that most Canadians don't really mean for them to work. The extreme version of this perspective is that Canada is (and perhaps always will be) a hostile, racist land full of people who want immigrants to do the heavy lifting while a clubby elite, overwhelmingly of European origin, continues to occupy the boardrooms, the legislatures, and the nice neighbourhoods. For these people, the idea that Canada's cities are plagued with ghettos full of struggling newcomers who face constant exclusion and discrimination, that immigrant and second-generation young people are seething with alienation and resentment, that newcomers aren't "adapting" to Canadian life because the majority of Canadians simply refuse to let them participate fully … well, it all makes perfect sense. The fact that efforts to integrate newcomers into such a systemically discriminatory society are failing is, if regrettable, satisfyingly predictable.

In other words, whatever you think *should* be happening with newcomers to Canada, the notion that the reality falls far short of the ideal proves you right. We regret to inform you that we have consensus: things are very bad. This standard-issue Canadian pessimism isn't entirely surprising, nor is it entirely unhelpful: thinking that things are going badly often means you're thinking about ways to try to make them go better. But there's a balance to be struck; excessive pessimism can lead to paralysis—or backlash.

It's pretty well conventional wisdom, at least among sociobiologists and their popularizers, that we humans are coded to sense danger. Evolution, or if you're so inclined, intelligent design, has programmed us to sense and respond to danger signals in order to enhance our chances of survival. Our capacity to receive and react to negative feedback from our environment is crucial to our individual and collective well-being. We need to absorb—even seek out!—bad news. Knowing that things are a little bit bad now ("I sense there's a lion nearby; I feel anxious …") may help us avoid their getting much worse in the future ("Ow! A lion is eating my foot!").

On the other hand, we don't need scientists to tell us that human beings also thrive on a sense of competence, confidence, trust, and purpose. We require at least *some* positive feedback if we're to hold our heads up. Suppose you're a kid and you get all Fs on your report card. As you're contemplating the wreckage, someone takes you aside and says that although you're probably incapable of it, you should maybe aim for one C next semester. What are the chances you'll even try?

We moderns are flooded with negative feedback thanks to our various communications technologies. For as long as we've had journalism we've had a steady diet of bad news, of course. But as our own Marshall McLuhan told us with famous prescience a generation ago, the global village condemns us forever to involvement with one another. And so in today's global media world, we don't just have *our* bad news, we have everyone's bad news—with pictures. We don't just read about thousands of people being drowned by accident or slaughtered on purpose, we see individual faces full of suffering and despair. We have only to flick on the television or open the newspaper to be fairly certain that the world is going to hell in a handbasket and taking us with it.

Canadians seem to expect, if not downright savour, bad news. Geographically big but psychologically small, Canada is populated by people who are highly attentive to the (bad) news in our country and the bad news from everywhere else. Sometimes I think it's a marvel we get out of bed in the morning to face such a troubled world. Of course, one reason we *do* get out of bed is that our lived reality tends to be much better than the world depicted in the media—but we tend to chalk the disjunction up to our own luck and our naïveté.

I am by no means a Pollyanna. I am a pollster. And like any good Canadian, I see plenty to worry about in the world—and also here in Canada. Still, even as we strive to confront the problems our country faces, it's crucial that we contextualize these problems—both historically and internationally—and acknowledge the ways in which things are going well. If we're serious about improving the lot of newcomers to this country and building a stronger Canada, then ignoring our successes is as bad as ignoring our failures. And so the task of this book is to provide, without trivializing the scale of our challenges, what I hope will be a useful corrective to the flood of negative news in the matrix of our media.

As a human being who wishes to survive and deeply wants his own children to not just survive but to thrive in this country or wherever they choose to live, I set out to learn how much of the negative feedback I was hearing in the media was true and how much was hype, misplaced fear of "the other" based on bad news from elsewhere, erroneous stereotypes, and other sloppy thinking that in the end won't enhance our chances of survival but, I believe, actually make things worse. And I admit that, contrary to the spirit of science, I was hoping that the news might not all be bad. I hoped that maybe in this as in so many areas of life Canadians would be muddling through, discovering step by incremental step a "Canadian way," unique in all the world, not destined to failure but somehow (sometimes implausibly) heading in the direction of success.

THE SUBTITLE of this book is *The Surprising Triumph of Canadian Pluralism*. Thus far I've gestured to some of the ways in which I hope to demonstrate that pluralism in this country is indeed a triumph—or at least a triumph in the making. Now I'd like to reflect on why this triumph is so surprising. For those of us who live in major Canadian cities, the peaceful coexistence of literally scores of different ethnocultural and linguistic groups is so much part of daily life that it's hard to imagine how much time and change it took to arrive at our present circumstances—both our demographics and our attitudes. From this country's early days, it was certainly not clear that Canada was on track to become the most multicultural country on earth, with the most favourable attitudes to immigrants from all over the world.

The founding racism of Canada, and indeed of the New (to Europeans) World, was of course racism against Aboriginal people. The displacement and betrayal of those who occupied the land that was to become Canada is a wrong that continues to haunt this country. As of the writing of these words in spring 2007, disputes over First Nations land claims threaten to disrupt transportation in Ontario as some Aboriginals conclude that the bureaucracy and, according to some, dishonesty of government-sanctioned processes are intractable. Compensation for those who were grossly abused in church-run residential schools just a generation ago has only recently been rolled out. And nothing can excuse the breathtaking finding that First Nations youth in this country are more likely to commit suicide than attend university. I believe, and I hope, that change may be afoot as an increasing diversity of thoughtful, forward-looking voices emerges from among the First Nations, but for now the plight of many Aboriginals in Canada serves as a reminder of at least a portion of the long history of racism in this country—and also of the power of complacency to forestall even the most urgently needed change.

Often when people talk about the colonization of the New World and the displacement or genocide of Aboriginal people, they describe "European" incursions. From the perspective of Aboriginals or anyone later attempting to imagine their experience, whether the colonizers were British, French, or Spanish is immaterial. But to Europeans themselves, of course, these differences were anything but irrelevant. The colonizers certainly didn't see themselves as part of Team Europe; they were trying to claim land for their own particular kings, queens, and countries. Explorers, soldiers, and settlers from *other* European countries were as inimical to their interests as Aboriginal peoples were.

In Canada, as any grade-five student knows, the British and French fought many wars over which colonizing force would lay claim to the new territory. And once the British had become the dominant ethnic and political group in Canada and realized they needed a lot of help settling the place, they were ready to begin exercising racism against not only Aboriginals and French-speaking settlers but against other European "races" too. Of course, contemporary science has shown that races don't exist at all at the level of our genes. Some groups of people share some genetic characteristics, but when you take into account regional variations within given races, interracial mixing both contemporary and historical, and other factors, the categories colloquially known as "races" simply collapse into one another. As the T-shirt says, Baby, we're all just animals.

But the fact that science would one day declare that no clear genetic break exists between, say, a Swede with pale skin, a Kenyan with dark brown skin, and an Iraqi with tan skin certainly didn't keep (British) Canadians in the late nineteenth and early twentieth centuries from pronouncing on the vast differences among the "Hebrews," the "Levantine races," the "Slavic races," and so on. I draw these categories from chapter headings in J.S. Woodsworth's 1909 book, *Strangers Within Our Gates*.[2] In this volume on Canadian immigration, Woodsworth, who became the first leader of the socialist

Co-operative Commonwealth Federation (CCF) and a hero of progressive Canadian politics, expounds upon the kinds of immigrants that would be good for Canada and the kinds that simply wouldn't do.

Good news for the Jews: "Naturally religious, temperate, home-loving, intelligent, industrious and ambitious, the Jew is bound to succeed," Woodsworth wrote. Italians also received largely favourable ratings, being "gay and light-hearted," but were "in danger of substituting beer for the light wines to which they are accustomed." Armenians were unfortunately "physically incapable of hard manual labour" in Woodsworth's view but served well as "pedlars or shop keepers." At least the Armenian wasn't the "unspeakable Turk."

As he moves beyond Europe, Woodsworth's racism trots to a gallop. For most European immigrants, his question is how the British elite will make the best use of their "natural" capabilities. But as to the Chinese and Japanese, he can only sigh that "the Oriental problem is not a new one in Canada." Woodsworth is so dismayed by the presence of people from East Asia on Canadian soil that he verges on the suggestion that it wasn't worth importing Chinese labourers to work on the Canadian Pacific Railway "when it was next to impossible to secure white labour." This was the state of immigration discourse a mere hundred years ago; indeed, Woodsworth's was seen as an enlightened voice.

Woodsworth's reference to Chinese labour on the CPR introduces another inglorious and well-known chapter of Canadian history. When he remarks that it was impossible to secure white labour, he neglects to mention that this was because work on the railway in western Canada was not only back-breaking but deadly. Many Chinese labourers were hired to complete tasks (often using explosives to blast passages through solid rock) that were so perilous no one wanted to risk white lives on them; nearly one in ten Chinese labourers hired to work on the railway was killed in the process. After all the necessary blasts were complete and the last spike was driven home, it seemed that some Chinese migrants still wished to come to Canada—hence the imposition of the head tax for which our federal government has only recently apologized and offered some restitution.

Of course, immigration wasn't the only arena in which bigotry was displayed in Canada. There were the anti-Semitic riots in Toronto's Christie Pits in 1933, preceded by the efforts by some Toronto residents to have Jews banned from the city's beaches. There was the internment of Japanese Canadians during World War II. There was the infamous declaration by a senior Canadian official that when it came to Canada's accepting Jews leaving Europe in the wake of the Holocaust, "none is too many." In Canada's centennial year, 1967, Africville, a black neighbourhood in Halifax that had existed longer than Canada itself, was simply bulldozed, partly to make room for a bridge, but clearly also because its residents' voices were of such minimal interest to decision-makers. These incidents, along with plenty of quotidian discrimination, scattered violence, and even some popular support for the kind of fascism that emerged more potently in Europe in the 1920s and 30s, speak to a Canadian history that is certainly not without the scourge of bigotry.

I raise this very brief sketch of Canadian racism not in an effort to make contemporary Canada seem angelic by comparison but to show how much change has occurred over time—and how unlikely it would once have seemed that Canada would even *aspire* to genuine, substantive equality for newcomers, let alone achieve it. It was only in the 1960s that Canada abandoned explicitly racist immigration policies and began admitting newcomers according to their skills and qualifications rather than their nations of origin. And while Canada, like all societies, remains imperfect, it has somehow evolved from the country J.S. Woodsworth once sought to protect from racial taint into the country we know today: a country with the highest immigration rate on the planet, where immigration—today 60 percent comes from Asia—is scarcely even *mentioned* in election campaigns, except in discussions of how the system can be refined and (most recently) how immigrants' qualifications can be better recognized in the Canadian economic system.

Historical perspective can sometimes be used as an apology for unacceptable present-day injustice. Looking at the gross economic inequality between blacks and whites in the United States, plenty of people shrug that it will "take time" for blacks to recover from slavery and segregation. Read: there's no need for anyone to take action; time will take care of it. But historical perspective can also serve as a reasonable corrective to the worries of the present in the same way empirical data can serve as a corrective to the alarming headlines of anecdotal evidence in the morning paper. Whenever a shooting occurs in Toronto, the papers tell us—implicitly if not outright—that Torontonians live in a tremendously dangerous city. And yet by any measure Toronto is an exceptionally safe city. It is so safe, in fact, that Torontonians hear about and lament (as well we should) every young life lost to gun violence in this town. While the deaths themselves are the worst possible news, the fact that individual deaths from violence make the front page in Toronto is *good* news. It means that they're not so commonplace as to go unreported.

Similarly, when we hear about foreign-born neurosurgeons driving taxis and engineers flipping burgers, we imagine that our dysfunctional system is probably beyond repair. But while these circumstances are unacceptable and deserve focused attention, Canadians should have a clear sense of the scale of the problem, the progress made to date, and the social resources available to improve things. As it turns out, those social resources—in the form of Canadians' belief in equality for all, their goodwill toward newcomers, their openness to difference—are considerable.

This book is an optimistic take on Canadian multiculturalism. It describes a work in progress, which will never be complete. It is about a society—from the longest-resident WASP family to the people arriving at Pearson, Trudeau, and Vancouver International at this very minute—that's doing a pretty good job at something no one has ever tried before. This book attempts to offer a balanced picture of what's happening in this country while encouraging neither complacency nor defeatism. This book wishes Canada well.

one

Immigration, Multiculturalism, and Canadian Identity

Nobody here, he is from Canada. So nobody can say,
"You could not be here. You cannot come."

—Toronto taxi driver, quoted by Pico Iyer in *The Global Soul*

So which is it? Are Canadians the most insecure people on the planet or the most arrogant? Canada's self-image is a curious thing. On the one hand, we think of ourselves as endlessly self-effacing: without a clear sense of what defines us as a nation; devoid of both European gravitas and American swagger; the kind of quivering people who apologize when someone steps on our toes.

On the other hand, Canadians are sometimes accused—not always unjustly—of being a little smug. In early 2005 the Pew Research Center, a major international survey research organization based in Washington, D.C., polled the citizens of sixteen countries on their attitudes toward a variety of international topics. Among other things, Pew's survey asked people how they thought their own country was perceived by the rest of the world. In France, a nation not renowned for its modesty, eight in ten thought the rest of the world perceived their country in a favourable light. In the United States, a country not infrequently accused of arrogance on the international scene, 84 percent thought the rest of the world had a positive impression of America. But Canada's chest puffed out farthest of all: 94 percent of Canadians reported that they figured the rest of the world admired their country.[1] (So much for our terminal self-effacement.)

(Traditionally, a good Canadian would have expected some kind of comeuppance for this shocking display of national hubris. Said comeuppance certainly did *not* come in the form of the 2007 survey GlobeScan conducted in twenty-seven countries on behalf of the BBC World Service, which found that on balance Canada was indeed the most highly regarded country on the planet.)[2]

If Canadians seem to have rather a high opinion of themselves, it's not because they're under any illusions about being the richest, the strongest, or the most influential country on earth. Rather, Canadians generally believe themselves to be peaceable and humane. And they like to think that if they're not as extrovertedly friendly as their American cousins, then they're deep-down nice in a quiet, unpretentious sort of way.

Above all, Canadians believe they participate in a just society, one that's respectful of diversity and mindful of vulnerability. These values lie at the heart of our deep attachment to our public health care system, our passion about our Charter of Rights and Freedoms, and our support for high rates of immigration and robust multiculturalism. But despite these policies, which most Canadians strongly support, we're loath to believe we're actually *experts* in anything. We value our public health care system, but even its most ardent defenders wouldn't call it the best in the world. We value our Charter, but it has been a contentious document and lacks the almost sacred dimensions of the U.S. Constitution, which stirs one's humanity from its opening line, "We hold these truths to be self-evident...." As for immigration and multiculturalism, if you read the daily papers—or even speak to your neighbours who've read the daily papers—you probably have the impression that most Canadians think we're doing it all wrong.

There has been a great deal of debate recently, both in Canada and abroad, about diverse societies and how—even whether—they can work. Britons were deeply shaken by the July 2005 terrorist attacks on the London transit system. On the morning of 7 July four young men, with large backpacks of the kind all young travellers seem to wear, boarded subway trains and a city bus. As the world was soon to learn, those backpacks were laden with explosives that would cause the deaths of fifty-two civilians. The four perpetrators hadn't just arrived from the hills of Tora Bora or any other foreign landscape; they'd come by car and train from northern England, where they had all grown up. (One of the four was born in

Jamaica but immigrated with his mother at the age of one.) But while the four men had spent almost all their lives in the UK, they were so disconnected from—indeed, hateful of—their fellow citizens that they chose to murder dozens of them in the name of religious extremism. Over the ensuing months, arrests of more would-be terrorists living in Britain heightened the sense that some of the country's minority groups, encouraged by multiculturalism to sustain their religious and cultural identities, were cut off from British society in ways that were proving disastrous.

Responding to concerns that violent religious extremism was being abetted by multiculturalism in some quarters of the country, Prime Minister Tony Blair gave a speech in December 2006 emphasizing the idea that for migrants and minority religious groups the "right to be different" must be decidedly balanced by a "duty to integrate." Although Blair stated that his speech was an articulation—not an abandonment—of British multiculturalism, London's *Telegraph* nevertheless reported that "Tony Blair formally declared Britain's multicultural experiment over yesterday."[3] Responding to officials' remarks on another multicultural matter two months earlier, *The Economist* agreed that a reversal was afoot: "The government now believes that Britain has struck the wrong balance between the tolerance of cultural diversity and the need for minority communities to integrate with wider society."[4]

In France, it wasn't terrorist attacks but mass riots that broadcast the unmistakable fact: deep fissures had developed in French society, largely along ethnic lines. On 27 October 2005 two young residents of the Paris suburb of Clichy-Sous-Bois were electrocuted. Some controversy exists over whether the youths—Zyed Benna, a seventeen-year-old of Tunisian origin, and Bouna Traoré, a fifteen-year-old of Malian origin—were being chased by police when they fled into a power station, but it seems likely that they believed they were. What is clear is that when the neighbourhood learned of the circumstances of their deaths, it exploded—and ignited similar explosions throughout France. *Le Monde* reported that the ensuing three weeks of violence saw the burning of nearly ten thousand vehicles and attacks on more than five hundred schools and other public buildings.

The deaths of Benna and Traoré seemed to unleash a wave of rage and resentment from thousands of young people, particularly those of North African origin, not just over their treatment by police but over their marginalization in French society. Unemployment rates are markedly higher among North Africans, and the activist group SOS Racisme has documented widespread employment discrimination against people with Muslim-sounding names. The election of Nicolas Sarkozy as French president in 2007 will have unknown implications for the lives of ethnic minority youth in the country. Sarkozy is himself the son of immigrants (from Hungary) and favours affirmative action to help non-white youth gain ground in education and employment. But Sarkozy is hardly an I-feel-your-pain kind of leader: after becoming interior minister, he eliminated community policing programs in poor suburbs, and even scolded police for organizing soccer matches with young people. "You are not social workers," he said. The language Sarkozy has used to discuss youth who break rules also speaks to a certain lack of patience with the frustrations of discrimination: he has called young petty criminals "thugs" and "scum" and declared that he would clear one Paris suburb of its restive youth with a high-powered hose.[5] Sarkozy, perhaps in a bid to head off charges of xenophobia, has appointed people with roots outside France to some high-ranking positions; his minister of justice, Rachida Dati, is a woman of North African origin who grew up in a housing project in Burgundy. Some believe that such moves early in Sarkozy's term are superficial gestures that will do little to improve relations between marginalized minority youth and the government mainstream French society has elected.

In Canada, we look at great countries like France and Great Britain struggling with their internal diversity and think, If these titans can't do it, we don't have a hope. What we fail to see is that if there's one area in which Canada can truly be called a global expert, it's in managing diversity. For sure we lack the flag-waving American patriotism or the French joie de vivre or the British stiff upper lip. But when it comes to welcoming newcomers from around the world and incorporating them into a new society, it turns out that none of those celebrated national traits seems to be a magic bullet; whatever it is we *do* have is what seems to be working best. Which is not to say that Canada is working perfectly. But whether we realize it or not, people in the countries we admire (and whose fine qualities cause us considerable insecurity) look to Canada when they seek lessons in managing diversity. To paraphrase Winston Churchill, we are the most racist, xenophobic, segregated society on earth, except for all the others.

Canada has often thought of itself as an ersatz version of other places. We were once (in the dominant national imaginary) an appendage of Great Britain: we sang for the Queen and fought alongside our colonial homeland in South Africa and in the Great Wars, but our architecture was less majestic, our tea wasn't as good, and—P.S.—we were half French. More recently, we've seen ourselves as a wannabe United States: also of British political heritage, also of the New World, but not as strong, not as rich, not as self-assured, and—P.S.—we're half French. But as time goes by, Canada is becoming less and less like these other places and more and more itself. And this evolution is owing in no small measure to this country's ever increasing internal diversity.

Will Kymlicka, a professor of philosophy at Queen's University and one of the world's leading authorities on multiculturalism, points out that Canada is not alone in being home to a diverse population, or even in addressing that diversity with something it labels "multiculturalism." Like Great Britain, Belgium, Spain, and many other countries, Canada has a national minority group: the Québécois. Like New Zealand, Australia, and countries throughout the Americas, Canada also has a significant Aboriginal population. And like Australia, the United States, and Germany, a large proportion of Canada's population is foreign-born. But Canada is the only place on earth that has all three of these characteristics: a national minority group, an Aboriginal population, and a substantial immigrant population.[6]

Multiculturalism, in this country and elsewhere, is often discussed in the vaguest terms. When people talk about multiculturalism, they sometimes just mean immigration from non-European countries: the mere presence of minority ethnic groups in Canada, Australia, the United States, or Western Europe. When many Canadians talk about multiculturalism, they imagine the multiculturalism policies of the 1970s and 80s. A favourite cliché is to complain about the funding of Ukrainian folk-dancing festivals—the kinds of heritage-preserving activities the federal government once supported but long ago ceased financing. Another thing people sometimes mean when they talk about multiculturalism is moral relativism: the idea that anyone can defend any behaviour at all with the claim that it's important to his or her "heritage" or "culture." This is the definition most often derided in the United States, where feminism, gay rights, disability rights, and all manner of social and political movements are lumped into the category of "multiculturalism." To some critics of this catch-all multiculturalism, the term connotes a culture of grievance, entitlement, and complaint. A multiculturalism gone mad.

Because the definition tends to be so slippery, it's easy to blame multiculturalism for any social ill. Creeping racial segregation? Blame multiculturalism. Gangs in schools? Diminished civic engagement? Global terror? Must have something to do with multiculturalism, the doctrine that tells people to cleave only to their own tribes or religious sects and not participate in any larger social group—unless they have a complaint or a request for funding.

These kinds of assumptions, if they hold true anywhere, grossly misrepresent the Canadian approach to multiculturalism. In Canada, multiculturalism has *always* been geared toward helping minority groups participate more fully in Canadian society—not to helping them opt out. The original multiculturalism framework had four goals. Three of these had to do with promoting shared citizenship and communication among groups; only one had to do with helping groups sustain their own identities. It is either a profound misunderstanding or a deliberate misrepresentation of the framework when a *National Post* editorial describes multiculturalism as "a policy that only feeds intolerance and misunderstanding by separating people into ethnic and racial tribes, formalizing—indeed celebrating—divisions."[7]

The idea that Canada needs to stop encouraging ethno-cultural segregation and start encouraging integration is something that has already occurred to the country's political leaders; indeed, it occurred to—and was advanced by—the very people who were the architects of this country's multiculturalism policy. When Prime Minister Pierre Trudeau introduced official multiculturalism in his 1971 speech to Parliament, he outlined four ways in which the government would support this new idea:

> First, resources permitting, the government will seek to assist all Canadian cultural groups that have demonstrated a desire and effort to continue to develop a capacity to grow and contribute to Canada, and a clear need for assistance, the small and weak groups no less than the strong and highly organized.
>
> Second, the government will assist members of all cultural groups to overcome cultural barriers to full participation in Canadian society.

Third, the government will promote creative encounters and interchange among all Canadian cultural groups in the interest of national unity.

Fourth, the government will continue to assist immigrants to acquire at least one of Canada's official languages in order to become full participants in Canadian society.[8]

If anyone snickered at the phrase "resources permitting," imagining that multiculturalism has come to consume a vast amount of funds, take comfort: Canadians talk a great deal about multiculturalism but spend very little on it. Of a total annual budget of $189 billion, about $27 million is earmarked for multiculturalism. In other words, it accounts for less than one-fiftieth of a percent of federal spending. (To put this in perspective, some other things the federal government has spent $27 million on in the past few years include the building of a soccer stadium in downtown Toronto; internship programs for young people in the Nipissing-Timiskaming region; and providing measles vaccinations to children in poor countries. All worthy projects no doubt, but their relatively small reach shows us that multiculturalism is hardly being funded on a grand scale relative to other government initiatives.) And most of the funds devoted to "multiculturalism" these days are directed toward efforts to combat discrimination against people based on their ethnic identity or their newcomer status.

Despite the program's meagre funding, however, it remains true that something unique is afoot in the relationship between Canadian society at large and minority ethnocultural groups, including newcomers. International public opinion data provide abundant evidence that in matters of immigration and multiculturalism, Canada is a very special case indeed.

CANADIAN OPENNESS TO IMMIGRATION

Canadians consistently express the most positive attitudes in the world toward immigration. In 2006 an international Ipsos MORI study found that 75 percent of Canadians believe that overall, immigrants have a positive influence on the country. The country with the second most positive attitudes, Australia, was slightly over half (54 percent), with the United States not far behind (52 percent). In Western Europe, Germans (47 percent) were the most positive about immigrants' influence on their country, with Spain (45 percent), France (45 percent), Italy (44 percent), and Great Britain (43 percent) hovering just below.

Especially striking are the "net positive" results—the number of points by which positive attitudes toward immigrants exceed negative attitudes in each country. Australia, for example—with 54 percent saying that immigrants overall have a positive effect on the country and 39 percent saying they have a negative influence—registers a net positive attitude of 15 percent. The table on page 15 shows the other countries surveyed as well. Canada, with a net positive attitude of 55 percent, ranks a full forty points higher than the next most positive country.[9]

Some observers claim that Americans, who, like Canadians, think of their country as a nation of immigrants, would be more positive about immigration if they weren't so challenged by the flow of illegal migrants from Mexico. The Mexican border and its attendant issues is surely the driving force behind any American wariness about immigration, the argument goes. But a look at the numbers reveals that Mexico doesn't explain the whole attitudinal difference between Canada and the United States. The 2005 Pew Global Attitudes Project cited earlier also surveyed a number of countries about their attitudes toward immigration from specific parts of the world. True, when asked whether immigration from Mexico and Latin America was good for their country, Canadians (78 percent) are markedly more likely than Americans (60 percent) to answer in the affirmative. But a similar difference emerges when Canadians and Americans are asked about immigrants from Asia: 77 percent of Canadians

Immigrant Influence

Q. Overall, would you say immigrants are having a good or bad influence on the way things are going in [country]?

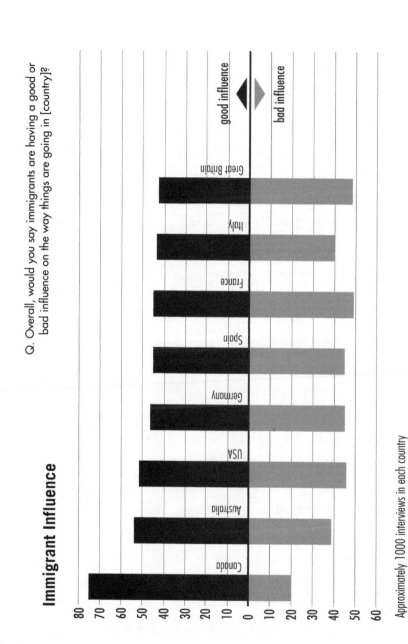

Approximately 1000 interviews in each country

SOURCE: "ATTITUDES TOWARD IMMIGRANTS," INTERNATIONAL SOCIAL TRENDS MONITOR, IPSOS MORI, MAY 2006, WWW.IPSOS-MORI.COM/ISTU/ISTU-MAY06.PDF

and 62 percent of Americans believe that immigration from Asia is a good thing for their respective countries. The United States doesn't share a long desert border with any Asian country, and yet Americans are no more likely to take a positive view of immigration from Asia than from Mexico. Perhaps geography isn't the whole story.

Over time immigration and ethnocultural diversity have become more central to the way Canadians think about their country. Indeed, as immigration rates have increased, the proportion of Canadians believing there is too much immigration to this country has actually diminished. In 1977, when Canada's immigration rate was only five thousand per million population, about two-thirds of Canadians believed the rate was too high, while about a third were satisfied.[10] Today those proportions are roughly reversed: as of 2006 only about a third of Canadians believe there is too much immigration to this country, while about two-thirds think it's about right or too low. Recall that at present Canada has the highest immigration rate in the world: seventy-seven hundred per million population. Even given this exceptional practice, Canada achieves a level of consensus about immigration that many countries with lower rates of intake can only dream of.

One common anti-immigrant sentiment is the idea that immigrants come to a new country and take jobs from the native-born. Most Canadians aren't buying that old saw. As of

2006, nearly three-quarters (73 percent) believe that overall immigrants have a positive effect on the Canadian economy. Just a quarter (24 percent) believe that immigrants take jobs away from other Canadians.

It's true that Canadians have some concerns about the way the immigration and refugee system is administered: only a minority (40 percent) agree that the existing system does a good job of keeping criminals and suspected criminals out of Canada, and a slim majority (54 percent) believe that many refugee claims aren't legitimate. (Notably, suspicion of refugee claimants is highest among immigrants themselves, who may suspect that others managed to jump the queue in which they themselves waited honestly for months or years.) But these perceived flaws of the system clearly do not undercut Canadians' belief in the overall project of accepting a quarter-million newcomers to our shores every year.

Moreover, the fact that Canadians believe their own immigration system to be flawed doesn't translate into negative opinions of immigrants themselves. For example, although only a minority believe that the system is good at keeping criminals out of the country, Canadians see that as a problem with the system, not with most newcomers: only 15 percent believe that immigrants commit more crime than native-born Canadians. In fact, in a survey of eight Western countries, Canadians were the least likely to see immigrants as more prone to criminal behaviour—less likely than Americans (19 percent), Australians (22 percent), Britons (25 percent), French (26 percent), Germans (35 percent), Spaniards (40 percent), or Italians (41 percent).[11]

Most Canadians continue to believe that the country's ambitious immigration policies are a good idea, if in need of some adjustments, and that the hundreds of thousands of new Canadians who come here each year mostly prove a boon to their adoptive home. This makes Canadians particularly well suited to the global context in which they find themselves: we live in a world that's on the move. According to the 2005 report of the Global Commission on International Migration, there were nearly 200 million international migrants in 2005.[12] One in thirty-five people on this planet has lived outside their native country for more than a year, a proportion that has increased by over 250 percent since 1970. The flow of people, goods, and ideas around the world is occurring at an unprecedented rate. And Canada has been in a kind of training for today's world since its birth. Most Canadians are at ease in a diverse society and implicitly recognize the need for immigrants in order to keep the country going. The most loudly touted projection of the 2006 Canadian census was that by 2030, Canada's population growth may be accounted for *exclusively* by immigration. This is a truly massive change that will require robust leadership from Canadian institutions. But the foundation from which Canada sets out on this project is perhaps the strongest in the world.

MULTICULTURALISM AND CANADIAN IDENTITY

In the speech that introduced official multiculturalism to Canadians in 1971, Prime Minister Trudeau laid out an aspiration of equality amid diversity. Significantly, he suggested that Canadians already sensed the necessity of a set of policies that would comprehend the diversity of the Canadian population, a population that comprised not only Aboriginal peoples and a national minority (the Québécois) but also a significant non-British, non-French immigrant population. In discussing "The Cultural Contributions of Other Groups," Volume IV of the report of the Royal Commission on Bilingualism and Biculturalism, Trudeau said,

It was the view of the royal commission, shared by the government and, I am sure, by all Canadians, that there cannot be one cultural policy for Canadians of British and French origin, another for the original peoples and yet a third for all others. For although there are two official languages, there is no official culture, nor does any ethnic group take precedence over any other. No citizen or group of citizens is other than Canadian, and all should be treated fairly.

In the years since Trudeau spoke those words, multiculturalism has become central to Canadians' sense of themselves and their country. In 2003, 85 percent of Canadians said that multiculturalism was important to Canadian identity. More Canadians cite multiculturalism as central to the national identity than bilingualism or hockey. Also in 2003, four out of five Canadians (81 percent) agreed that multiculturalism has contributed positively to the national identity. When Jonathan Kay writes in the *National Post,* in an opinion piece titled "Multiculturalism, R.I.P. (1982–2007)," that "most of us think the whole idea [of multiculturalism] is nonsense,"[13] he may mean most of "us *National Post* columnists" or most of his friends—because if he means most of "us Canadians," he is mistaken.

Not only do Canadians feel that multiculturalism is a central part of their country's identity, it's also increasingly a source of pride. In 1985 we asked Canadians to tell us in their own words what made them proud to be Canadian. Multiculturalism was in tenth place. People were more likely to cite the beauty of the land, Canada's natural resources, and even the physical size of the country. By 2006, though, multiculturalism had climbed to second place. Only

Canada's democracy was more often named as a source of national pride.

Immigrants themselves are especially likely to derive pride from Canada's multiculturalism and to feel that it's an important part of Canada's identity. But at still only 19 percent of the population, immigrants are not the ones driving this trend; native-born Canadians increasingly see their country as being defined and enriched by its diversity and by the official response to that diversity: multiculturalism.

As Will Kymlicka puts it, Canadians aren't unique in living in a diverse society. Rather, "Canadians are distinctive in the way that they have incorporated Canada's policy of accommodating diversity into their sense of national identity."[14] Public opinion data certainly suggest that multiculturalism holds an ever more central position in the imagined community that is Canada.

FRETTING ABOUT MULTICULTURALISM

But of course, all is not well in the peaceable yet neurotic kingdom of Canada. Or at the very least, all is not perceived to be well. In a March 2006 article in *The Walrus* my fellow pollster Allan Gregg outlined some of the events, both domestic and international, that he believed were giving rise to concerns about the wisdom and success of our multicultural policies.[15]

As signs that diverse Western societies were in trouble, Gregg cited the July 2005 bombings of the London transit system by a handful of British-raised Muslim men and rioting in the suburbs of Paris by disaffected youth, largely of North African origin but also generally French-born. Gregg also pointed to an episode that made less of a splash in the international media but that was arguably of greater import to Canadians because it took place in Australia, a country often seen as Canada's twin on matters of immigration and multiculturalism.

It happened on a sunny Sunday afternoon in December 2005 on Cronulla beach, a popular oceanside spot in Sydney. Five thousand white Australian youth descended on the beach and perpetrated violent attacks on Lebanese beach-goers. The riot was sparked by an incident a week earlier in which Lebanese youth had assaulted a pair of lifeguards. Some observers denied that the riot was racist and saw the incidents at the beach more as clashes between rival gangs. But if they were gang fights, they were ethnic gang fights, with white youth chanting racist slogans and aiming to rid "their" beach of outsiders—even if those outsiders were born in Australia, as tens of thousands of Lebanese Australians were.

Gregg's article read as a warning. If strife—violent, murderous ethnic strife—hadn't yet seized Canada, he argued, it wasn't because Canada was any different from these other countries; it was because the immigrants who would one day grow restive hadn't yet gotten old enough, angry enough, disillusioned enough. Canada's immigrants and their children were still too new to the country. They were not yet so disgusted by their intractable marginalization in Canadian society that they wanted to lash out against their "host culture." But the day was coming, as inevitable as tomorrow's sunrise in the east. We had only to look at other Western countries with large migrant populations to see where this country was headed. If it could happen there, it would happen here.

A few months after his piece was published, proof emerged that Canada wasn't immune to the spectre of global terror—which, rightly or wrongly, has become bound up in discourse about immigration and multiculturalism. Eighteen men and boys in the Greater Toronto Area were arrested on suspicion of plotting terrorist attacks on Canadian targets. According to media reports, the men had acquired several tonnes of ammonium nitrate, a fertilizer that can be used in the creation of explosives. (The Oklahoma City bombing, for instance, was carried out using just one tonne of the substance.) Their alleged intention was to strike at Canadian civilians in locations of national prominence, including Parliament and the CBC headquarters in downtown Toronto.

Of the suspects who were adults (and whose identities could therefore be made public), most were in their early twenties and most had been born and raised in Toronto or its suburbs.

Some had emigrated from Pakistan or Somalia but had arrived in the country as young children. By and large the young men seem to have had quiet, middle-class backgrounds. But somewhere in these quiet lives twelve men (and several minors) allegedly became prepared to do violence to their Canadian compatriots in the name of Islam. The story went that if Canada had failed to convince them that life here was preferable to death in the name of an extremist ideology, then this country—with the highest immigration rates in the world and the second highest foreign-born population—was in deep trouble.

Other incidents also seemed to suggest simmering problems. In Montreal there was an outcry over the installation of some windows. Yes, windows. The Mile End neighbourhood of Montreal is home to a diverse collection of residents: immigrant retirees of Greek, Portuguese, and Italian origin; young families, both anglophone and francophone; university students who ride the bus across Mont-Royal to attend classes and then return to their friendly neighbourhood to study over coffee at one of the area's many independent cafés.

Mile End is also home to a bustling Hasidic Jewish community, which has established numerous thriving synagogues, yeshivas (religious schools), and businesses in the area. The Yetev Lev synagogue is situated directly behind the Park Avenue YMCA. In the spring of 2006 the leaders of the synagogue approached the YMCA with a concern and a proposal. The concern was that the students at the Yetev Lev yeshiva, mostly young men in their late teens, were being distracted by the sight of women in workout attire performing Pilates and other exertions in the YMCA's exercise room. The proposal was that the synagogue foot the $3500 bill to have the exercise room's windows replaced with frosted glass, which would let light in but keep arousing visions from seeping out. The YMCA's advisory committee accepted the proposal in a gesture of reasonable neighbourly accommodation.

In the ensuing months, however, a backlash emerged not only among YMCA members but throughout Quebec. Newspapers that covered the story were flooded with letters to the editor. The issue even came up during the Quebec provincial election in the spring of 2007; both Action Démocratique leader Mario Dumont and Liberal leader Jean Charest expressed disapproval of the YMCA's decision, indicating that too much ground had been ceded by a secular facility to meet the demands of a religious minority. Ultimately, the frosted glass was removed and replaced with transparent panes once again. But the most significant window in the case was the one onto a simmering resentment of religious minorities in the province: many Quebecers felt that the province's policy of "reasonable accommodation" of minority religious practices had become unreasonable: it had gone too far.

Montreal hasn't been the only hotspot for ethnic disputes in *la belle province* in the first sliver of the twenty-first century. Unlike the Mile End YMCA, the town council of Herouxville was in no mood for accommodation when it drew up its code of conduct for newcomers to its community of thirteen hundred souls, a document that received attention not only throughout Canada but from such international media outlets as the BBC and Fox News. Signed by the mayor and six town councillors, the code made explicit Herouxville's persistent celebration of Christmas, its modern practice of having boys and girls play and attend school together, and its residents' willingness to dance and drink alcohol in public. More pointedly, it advised all comers that in Herouxville it is frowned upon for women to be beaten to death or burned alive in public. Advocates of the document insisted that it was not targeted at any one group but was merely a statement of the town's character, designed to head off any problems that might arise from immigrants' misconceptions of Herouxville as a place where they might beat people to death with impunity. Among the reported inspirations for the document was the debate over the YMCA windows.

The Herouxville declaration was ridiculed in some quarters as the expression of a small town's hysteria about issues of which it had little direct experience. (Herouxville reportedly had one immigrant family at the time the declaration was written, and presumably others have not flocked there in the wake of the document's release.) But its defensive posture did indicate that some Canadians (particularly Quebecers) were feeling threatened by the social changes they perceived to be happening around them; one Herouxville town councillor even asked Premier Jean Charest to declare a state of "cultural emergency" in the province. Even if one assumed that Herouxville was under no serious threat of having public stonings on Main Street (or Rang St-Pierre, as the case may be), it was clear that cracks were beginning to appear in the traditional Canadian consensus that newcomers should be given the benefit of the doubt.

Other debates about reasonable accommodation emerged around an assortment of head scarves worn by an assortment of Muslim women. An eleven-year-old Muslim girl was ejected from a soccer game (by a punctilious Muslim referee) because her hijab (a head scarf that covers the hair but leaves the face exposed) was judged to be the kind of dangerous attire prohibited by the Fédération Internationale de Football Association (FIFA), the international body governing soccer. (FIFA officials, meanwhile, argued that there is no prohibition against hijabs and that Muslim footballers routinely wear hijabs during games in Europe.) Shortly thereafter, a Quebec correctional officer was given a choice: come to work without the hijab she normally wears or don't come in at all. She stayed home.

Most of these incidents, it bears noting, have transpired in Quebec—a distinct society with its own particular concerns about minority status. But anxiety about accommodating and relating to the diversity that has come to Canada over the last several decades does not exist only in *la belle province*. News stories and anecdotal data suggest that Canadians are in the process of questioning whether as a culture we're in over our heads: whether we can really foster diversity on this scale and in this manner without deleterious social consequences.

Public opinion data point in a similar direction. Since 1993 we've asked Canadians whether "too many immigrants do not adopt Canadian values." Agreement with this statement initially stood at 72 percent. Over time it declined gently but steadily, until in 2005 the proportion of Canadians agreeing with the statement had sunk to 58 percent. When we asked again in 2006, though, agreement had spiked by seven points to 65 percent. That is, two-thirds of Canadians were expressing anxiety about the cultural integration of newcomers. This finding may be an anomaly in a longer downward trend. But given that the period between the 2005 and 2006 surveys included many of the events I've just named—not to mention a good portion of the heated Ontario debate over provincial recognition of Sharia law—it seems likely that opinion genuinely shifted during this time and that the rapid uptick in the numbers isn't merely a blip. In short, Canadians have become more likely to agree with Allan Gregg that something about multiculturalism is broken and that immigrants aren't adequately adapting to life in Canada.

The question of whether newcomers are *in fact* integrating successfully has many facets: it encompasses the jobs immigrants find (or don't find), the neighbourhoods they live in (or don't), their feelings about Canada, and their engagement with the political life of their adoptive country. The question at hand, however, isn't so much how new Canadians are actually doing as how debates about immigration and multiculturalism are affecting all Canadians' attitudes about their country—a country, as I've shown, that they increasingly perceive as being defined by its diversity.

WHO DO WE THINK WE ARE?
(OR, THE PARADOX OF CANADIAN CHAUVINISM)

National identity, a thorny issue in Canada at the best of times, is among the topics of the moment even for such venerable and self-assured cultures as France, Great Britain, and the Netherlands, each of which once bragged of an empire. Canadians are used to sprawling, circular, who-are-we, where-is-here, what-does-it-all-mean debates; we express our existential angst with the regularity of a national menstrual cycle.

Sometimes we consider these threadbare questions with the help of television pundits, historians, or pollsters; at other times we rely on writers and filmmakers to tell us in their own ways that there's no here here (or maybe there is … but it's complicated. You'd better sit down). But for Canadians to watch *others* engage in these debates has been most unusual. The British in knots about Britishness? The French uncertain about Frenchness? The Dutch debating what it is to be Dutch? It seems that everyone is talking about how (or, in some quarters, *whether*) shared citizenship, a sense of common cause, trust, and genuine empathy with others, can be fostered in societies where people have diverse ethnocultural, political, and religious backgrounds. The academics fret about what they call declines in social capital or the erosion of social cohesion—jargon for the same phenomena.

Of course, while in Europe these discussions are being spurred largely by contemporary migration, in Canada they're older than the country itself. Canada never was a unitary entity. It was created in the presence of Aboriginal peoples (profoundly mistreated and displaced, but not annihilated by genocide—and therefore an abiding social and political presence) with the necessary engagement of two colonial peoples, British and French, and was hugely reliant on additional European immigration to settle the West, expand the railway across the continent, exploit the land's natural resources, and ultimately build our cities. Canadians have never been one people in one place; we've been a diverse people spread across a vast territory. Unlike the Americans, we made no defining political choice together (like a revolution) that would bind us more strongly than blood. A unitary Canadian identity is a national joke more than anything else. Any effort to craft and impose a single national narrative would be briefly debated but would soon devolve into a gag retold from sea to sea.

Because of this indeterminacy, some seem to feel that when it comes to the integration of newcomers, Canada doesn't have a chance. If people whose forebears arrived two centuries ago still haven't figured out a solid definition of what it means to be Canadian, how can Canada ask people arriving next week to pledge themselves to its cause? (*What* cause? Snow tires? Poutine? Bringing the Stanley Cup home?) With its immigration rates, foreign-born population, naturalization rates, and decades-old multicultural policy, Canada is obviously engaged in an unparalleled effort to foster diversity within its borders and fuel its population growth exclusively (as the most recent census projects) with people from elsewhere in the world. But who do we think we are? What do we think we're doing?

In his essay in *The Walrus*, Allan Gregg worried about Canadians' ability to find common ground in a multicultural society. Part of his worry seemed to stem from what he sees as a void at the heart of Canadian culture: the sense that at the centre of Canada's social imaginary, just as at its geographic middle, there's not much of a there there. Gregg argues that as a core identity, multiculturalism isn't going to cut it: "Some have suggested promoting diversity itself as a rallying call for all Canadians, but ... drawing attention to difference can undermine attempts to forge an overarching national identity." Gregg goes on to worry that "without grand designs or defining national projects, new immigrants run the risk of arriving and going about their business with little sense of the roles they can play in their adopted homeland. With no national mythology to adhere to, they naturally retreat to the familiar, seeking out their own communities."

Gregg is right to point out that national mythologies have fallen on hard times—and he's certainly not the only person to observe that Canada never enjoyed much of a heyday on those fronts anyway. But is it desirable for Canada to create or revive "grand designs" and "defining national projects" as a way of enticing newcomers to participate in their adoptive society? The Chinese who helped build the railway were part of a defining national project. They were worked into the ground building the infrastructure of a country in which they'd never be allowed to participate fully—even if they survived to see the last spike driven home. Clearly, participation in a national project isn't a sufficient condition for successful integration.

Nor, for that matter, is a clear idea of "the roles [newcomers] can play in their adopted homeland," as J.S. Woodworth's book demonstrated. Knowing how to make good use of "the thrifty, ambitious hardworking Scandinavians" or the "Galician ... working with a physical endurance bred of centuries of peasant life" is hardly the key to social cohesion in a postmodern, globalized world. I'm being somewhat facetious: obviously neither Allan Gregg nor any other serious commentator is proposing a return to the exploitative and nakedly racist immigration practices of the past, predicated on the idea that one's background defines one's future. My point in raising Woodsworth is simply that making strict and specific demands of newcomers in order that they might know the kind of society in which they're expected to participate—and what form that participation will take—isn't a new idea. It's an old idea that has, I'm happy to say, been almost universally rejected.

The contemporary version, of course, is that immigrants should be offered the same variety of social roles as any other Canadian: the same national ideals and aspirations; the same economic and social opportunities; the same freedoms, rights, and responsibilities. The criticism Gregg and others are making is that the give-and-take relationship between Canada and its new citizens is too nebulous—that in asking so little in terms of cultural identification and, yes, assimilation, Canada shortchanges both itself and its newcomers, allowing them to drift off into segregated ethnic communities for want of any reason to engage with the wider society.

In his book *The Unfinished Canadian,* Andrew Cohen worries that Canada is not only a segregated society—an "ethnic archipelago"—but a pit stop for a global tribe of rootless people who live here when convenient, take off when the weather gets bad, and don't give much of a damn about the 140 years of history that have brought this country to its current state (prosperous and peaceable but flawed in many, many other ways, Cohen warns).[16] He advises us that Canadian identity is becoming very flimsy indeed as people from around the world come to think of this country as a "hotel" (Yann Martel, who loves it), a "railway station" (George Jonas, who worries about it), or simply the convergence of "a hundred diasporas" (Pico Iyer, who savours it when he visits). Whether Cohen counts Canadians of European ancestry who spend their winters in Florida or Arizona among the ranks of unworthy fair-weather Canadians isn't clear. In listing the symptoms of our inadequate coherence as a nation he mentions only "Jamaican, Haitian, and other street gangs," "Indo-Canadian[s]," "Muslims," and "Somalis," and of course Canadian citizens who were evacuated from Lebanon during the 2006 Israeli bombing, who Cohen says treat Canada as a taxi service.

Is it true, as Cohen and Gregg argue in different ways, that some basic absence at the core of Canadian identity is no longer tenable in the face of an inflow of a quarter-million newcomers a year? Is our multiculturalism indeed, as political scientist Gad Horowitz once suggested, a "masochistic celebration of Canadian nothingness" that will only ever produce more nothingness—or, worse than nothingness, segregation, strife, and violence?[17] In order to successfully integrate newcomers into this society, must Canada formulate some kind of civics boot camp for native-born and foreign-born alike so that we all know exactly what it means to be Canadian? And will there be a test?

Looking at countries that do boast a powerful sense of common identity, it seems plain that such cohesion hasn't been of much use in helping minority groups feel like full members of the society. Many newcomers to France, for example—and even many children of newcomers—feel that the notion of Frenchness is *so* powerful, so remote, and indeed so Gallic and white that they can never be a part of it.

There are two things to note here. First, we can learn only so much about our own situation from other countries. As UBC geographer David Ley points out, it is neither helpful nor defensible to map other nations' crises uncritically onto the Canadian landscape:

Much contemporary popular writing is inspired by the cross-national transmission of media text and images that

selectively highlight points of crisis, presenting them as
normative, eliding significant differences in national
conditions, and sliding across thin ice in prescribing
causality. In this spontaneous and often uncritical transmission of tarnished ethnoscapes from elsewhere, multiculturalism has been projected as the abiding context, the
grab bag for all manner of policy failures.[18]

Second, to the extent that we *do* have a problem integrating newcomers, it's spurious to attribute this to the lack of a
firm identity. A country can have a strong sense of itself
indeed—and be no better (or much worse) at integrating
newcomers than a country that fumbles along trying merely
to populate its land, fuel its economy, and live up to its own
aspirations of equality, the rule of law, and the nonviolent
resolution of conflict. A sharply defined sense of "us" and
"them" and how to make "them" become more like "us" is in
no way a surefire means of achieving lasting and harmonious
integration.

It's true that Canadians have always had a bit of an identity problem. Judging by the traditional markers of nation-
hood—a shared ethnicity, religion, and heritage—we're all
over the historical and socio-cultural map. In the early part of
the twentieth century we at least cohered as a nation around
allegiances to the mother country (Britain) or our big brother

(the United States) when it came time to fight. But ever since Vietnam our willingness to go to war alongside America has ceased to be a given. Today, for example, the vast majority of Canadians believed Jean Chrétien was right to refuse to join the United States and Great Britain in the 2003 invasion of Iraq.

But in fostering a successful, diverse society, the lack of consensus on our national identity may be not an Achilles heel but rather our foot in the door, our unlikely secret weapon. At present, we ask newcomers to obey Canadian laws and learn a little about the country. Formally, we ask them to make the following pledge of citizenship: "From this day forward, I pledge my loyalty and allegiance to Canada and Her Majesty Elizabeth the Second, Queen of Canada. I promise to respect our country's rights and freedoms, to defend our democratic values, to faithfully observe our laws and fulfill my duties and obligations as a Canadian citizen." (One might add that many native-born Canadians would hold their noses or downright refuse to pledge their "loyalty and allegiance" to the Queen or anyone else they consider the head of a foreign country. But I digress.)

In cultural terms, however, newcomers make their own way. There's no great secret. There's no special quality—inherited or otherwise—that makes you fully Canadian. There's no royal jelly, no password, no secret handshake. This is the paradox of

Canadian chauvinism—the reason for both our smugness and our insecurity. We do suspect, deep down, that we're superior to other countries—precisely because we don't think we're superior. We don't imagine we possess some core identity worth forcing onto others, something essential that will be lost if we let newcomers retain their own customs. (Indeed, we tend to fear people and countries who think they have all the answers.) Rather, we have core values that evolve, partly in response to the diverse people we meet through the course of our lives. I believe most Canadians think that newcomers will probably make us better and more interesting over time. Indeed, three-quarters of Canadians agree with the statement, "Other cultures have a lot to teach us. Contact with them is enriching for us." Among young people aged fifteen to twenty-four, eight in ten (79 percent) agree with the statement. To them it's obvious.

If Anglo Canadians had been left to their own devices in this hostile land, we'd still be clearing brush in Manitoba, ending each back-breaking day with a meal of boiled beef, anxiously awaiting a royal visit or annexation into the great Republic.

Want to be Canadian? Check out our laws, and especially our Charter. If you can handle those, then live here, in a neighbourhood as diverse or as homogeneous as you choose, be it Herouxville in Quebec, Kensington Market in downtown

Toronto, a block of Richmond, B.C., that might as well be Hong Kong, a gay village, whatever—just get along.

As it turns out, almost everyone does.

IDENTITY CRISIS

If Canadians are so comfortable with our soft, chewy centre, why do we look worried? If we're so unthreatened by immigration and multiculturalism, why the proportionate spike in those who believe that too many immigrants aren't adopting "Canadian values"? Why the signs that in some quarters of the land, people feel a deep discomfort with the diversity we've claimed for years to be the country's very hallmark?

I believe that Canada, like some other Western countries, is indeed undergoing a kind of identity crisis. But not all identity crises are the same. For countries with a stronger sense of internal unity it's the spectre of difference that rings alarm bells. Can France be France when it can no longer ignore the thousands of disaffected minority youth in Paris suburbs? Can the traditional idea of Frenchness and today's reality be reconciled? Can Britain be Britain when it confronts the racial segregation of Leeds or Manchester? Can Holland be Holland, Germany Germany, Sweden Sweden? Most people hope so.

Can Canada be Canada in the awareness of diversity within its borders? Of course it can. It has never been otherwise. Let's even suppose that Canada in its early days—as it exiled Aboriginals to reserves and consigned Quebec (as far as it was able) to second-class status—wasn't truly reconciled to its internal diversity. Even if we accept that premise, we know that the first step toward the official multicultural doctrine of 1971 was the simple acknowledgment—the recognition— that Canada was already diverse. Not that it would step up immigration, not that it would adopt some new way of engaging minority communities in the future, but that it was *already* a pluralist society. This, the first phase of Canadian multiculturalism, before the funding for folk dancing and the anti-racism campaigns, has been called "demographic multiculturalism." It simply existed, and it was finally given a name. That is, to the extent that Canada was going to have a crisis about the mere fact of diversity, it happened more than three decades ago.

The current identity crisis isn't about whether white, European, Christian Canada can survive the presence of "Others." That question has long since been resolved. Rather, it's about whether our existing multiculturalism is a tenable ideal. Indeed, we seem to be worried about whether it counts as an ideal at all. Is Canada's multicultural project, seldom sharply defined and too often defended with clichés and bureaucratic jargon, actually something to strive for? Or is it merely a kind of nihilism: intellectually lazy, culturally self-loathing, politically cynical (with "ethnic votes" going to the highest bidder), and socially suicidal?

The data I've presented in this chapter suggest that Canadians *sense* that living in a diverse, just, and peaceful society is actually something to strive for. Canadians certainly don't perceive the current circumstances as perfect. I've already cited data indicating some Canadian anxiety about the integration of newcomers. Moreover, as of December 2006 large majorities of Canadians believed that a host of minority groups, including but not limited to Muslims (76 percent), Aboriginals (74 percent), South Asians (73 percent), and blacks (70 percent), experience at least occasional if not frequent discrimination.[19] (Statistics Canada's Ethnic Diversity Survey affirms that significant proportions of these minority communities do experience discrimination; our own survey of Canadian Muslims finds that about three in ten report a negative experience related to their race, religion, or ethnicity in the past two years.) But despite these and other problems, popular support for multiculturalism in this country remains both broad and deep. In other words, what is sometimes called the "multicultural experiment" isn't an experiment at all. It's a national aspiration at the very core of Canadian idealism. It's the Canadian Dream.

Canadians are indeed striving toward an increasingly diverse, peaceful, and just society. They may be doing so imperfectly, and yet with no small measure of goodwill and with considerable success. With domestic pundits so intent on pointing out flaws and warning signs, Canadians might be forgiven for being the last to know that in many ways we're on our way to becoming the planet's leading experts in the quiet heroism of getting along.

two

The Facts on the Ground

Everyone is entitled to his own opinion, but not his own facts.
—Daniel Patrick Moynihan,
United States senator and ambassador

ALTHOUGH A HOST OF POLLS show Canadians to be exceptionally positive about immigration to and diversity in their country, those numbers don't necessarily tell us anything about what's actually working or not working in newcomers' own experiences. Public opinion gives us only the aspirational part of the picture. So in this chapter I look beyond survey data and consider how migration and ethnic diversity are playing out in Canadian politics, cities, workplaces, and families.

ETHNIC ENCLAVES

The past few years have seen considerable discussion in the national media about what are being called ethnic enclaves. According to a 2004 Statistics Canada report, the number of these "ethnic enclaves"—defined as communities made up of

30 percent or more of a single visible minority group—had risen from 6 in 1981 to a whopping 254 in the 2001 census.[1] The report received some coverage at the time, but with Western countries' growing concern about integration, it has since gained legs.

For example, in early 2007 *The Globe and Mail* was reporting on the 2004 Statistics Canada study as though it were breaking news. The three-year-old report wasn't breaking news; rather, it was serving as handy fuel for Canadians' anxiety—in the wake of the arrests of the alleged would-be terrorists in Mississauga, Ontario, and assorted international crises that were read as relating to multiculturalism—about how minority groups were or were not participating in Canadian society. In a formulation common in Canadian media, Marina Jiménez wrote in the *Globe* that "Canada has the highest per capita immigration in the world—three times higher than the United States—and its geographic self-segregation of immigrants and their offspring could become an explosive issue. So far, the country has avoided the social upheaval underway in Europe, where riots struck the mainly Arab and African Paris suburbs two years ago."[2] That "so far" is ominous, and offers a striking example of what David Ley called the "often uncritical transmission of tarnished ethnoscapes from elsewhere."[3] Paris has a large ethnic minority population and so do Canadian cities; if cars burn in Clichy-Sous-Bois, we're told, we'd better alert our fire departments.

Much of the concern about ethnic enclaves in our cities is well intentioned. People are right to be worried about such issues as the concentration of poverty among particular ethnic groups (and as Jiménez points out, non-white families make up three-quarters of the country's poor). People are also right to worry about the segregation of Canadians with low incomes, of whatever race, in inhospitable neighbourhoods—particularly if it seems that people get stuck in these neighbourhoods over long periods, or even across generations.

What is *not* a good idea is to think about Canadian neighbourhoods in terms of neighbourhoods in other countries with vastly different demographic and policy realities from our own. Canada isn't free of racism, discrimination, poverty, or injustice. But the Canadian context *is* unique. Our history is different. Our policies are different. Our immigrant population is different. Our cities are different. Different from Europe, from the United States, from everywhere else on earth. And as the polls cited in chapter one attest, our national attitudes are different. In order to understand what's happening in Canada with respect to our immigration and multiculturalism policies, we have to consider Canada on its own terms—not as a potential footnote to events in France, Great Britain, the United States, or even Australia.

What do we really know about Canada's "ethnic enclaves"? And what, *if anything,* do these neighbourhoods tell us about what's working and not working about Canadian immigration and multiculturalism?

First, let's consider why people worry about these enclaves. Overall, concern seems to break out into two broad strains. One strain is that ethnic enclaves are places where people live because they can't live anywhere else: they arrive in Canada, settle where they know a few people (who likely share their nation of origin), struggle economically, face racism and other discrimination, and essentially remain stuck. Residents of these enclaves would like to move to another neighbourhood—one that may include better housing, better schools, more amenities, less crime, and greater diversity—but because of some combination of poverty, employment barriers, and housing discrimination, they stay where they are. In other words, people live in enclaves (or ghettos) because they're excluded.[4]

The second strain of concern relates to more affluent ethnic enclaves: enclaves of choice. One thinks of well-off Italians in Woodbridge, Ontario,[5] or Chinese in Richmond, B.C.— people who could live anywhere they wish, and choose to live among those who share the language and culture of their country of origin. Some fret that these enclaves become monocultural societies in themselves: places where minority groups opt out of the wider Canadian society, disengage politically, and hunker down with like-minded (or even just like-complexioned) neighbours.

The first kind of ethnic enclave is defined by a worrying lack of choice, the second by a worrying (to some) exercise of same. Jiménez's article in the *Globe* worries about both. In her reference to the Paris riots "so far" avoided in this country, she raises the spectre of the ghetto; later she gestures toward the freely chosen enclave: "Today, Canada seeks out immigrants with more money and earning power, and many bypass inner-city neighbourhoods and head straight for the suburbs."

Similarly, writing in the *Toronto Star* in March 2004 upon the release of the Statistics Canada report, Nicholas Keung quotes Usha George of the University of Toronto, who describes enclaves defined by poverty: "For a lot of [new immigrants], the congregations in certain neighbourhoods are not by choice. Most of them are forced to do it. It should raise some concerns to our policy-makers."[6] Keung also quotes Lucia Lo of York University, who remarks on enclaves defined by affluence: "Today, our immigrants are very different from those we used to get in the old days. They are much better educated. When they move to Canada, they don't restrain themselves to the dirty, filthy and crowded downtown ghettos. They want to live in a house with a full backyard in the suburbs."

It's certainly not impossible that both kinds of ethnic enclaves coexist in Canada. Still, the slippery terms in which they're discussed suggest that some commentators aren't quite sure what they're afraid of. The assumption seems to be that diverse neighbourhoods indicate social health while ethnically concentrated neighbourhoods indicate social trouble—whether it's exclusion of poor minority groups by the host culture or rejection of the host culture by more affluent minority groups. Either way, we're told, the problem is probably multiculturalism, which has encouraged us to focus on cultural diversity rather than on equality, and which has encouraged newcomer groups to shore up the cultural characteristics that differentiate them from other Canadians rather than seeking common ground and integration in daily life.

What is really happening in Canadian neighbourhoods, and, where things are going wrong, to what extent is multiculturalism to blame?

The census does affirm that an increasing number of neighbourhoods in Canadian cities contain concentrations of visible minority groups. But there is much evidence to suggest that this isn't a symptom of ghettoization so much as a result of the drastic increase in Canada's visible minority population over the past two and a half decades. According to the census, the proportion of the total Canadian population represented by visible minority groups rose from 4.7 percent in

1981 (1.1 million people) to 13.4 percent (4 million people) in 2001. Those three million people, mostly newcomers to Canada, have to live somewhere.

Disproportionately, of course, they live in Canadian cities. It's not necessarily a sign of racism or social exclusion that when they first arrive in Canada's cities, newcomers choose to live in neighbourhoods where people share their language and nation of origin. (Incidentally, Mohammad Qadeer, professor emeritus of urban planning at Queen's University, and Sandeep Kumar, professor of urban design at Ryerson University, find that language and nation of origin are much more salient than race in determining how ethnocultural communities cluster together.)[7] This has long been a common settlement pattern for those arriving in Canadian cities, and one that has resulted in some of this country's most celebrated neighbourhoods: Toronto's Kensington Market, Vancouver's Chinatown, and Montreal's Mile End neighbourhood, made famous by writer and raconteur Mordecai Richler.

The increased concentration of particular visible minority groups in Canadian neighbourhoods is *not,* then, a case of the growing segregation of long-time Canadians. It's a case of having more visible minority newcomers than ever before, and of those newcomers doing what newcomers of all races have always done: gone to the most familiar-feeling neighbourhoods in a new and unfamiliar land. Indeed, Feng Hou of Statistics Canada suggests that today's newcomers may even be *less* concentrated than were the newcomer groups of the past (groups such as Italians, Jews, Portuguese, and Greeks, whose concentration in "ethnic enclaves" is now less likely to incite a flurry of journalistic consternation than it is to inspire dinner reservations).[8] For example, Hou finds that in 1981 Italians represented about the same proportion of Toronto's population as South Asians did in 2001. And yet in 1981 a greater proportion of the city's neighbourhoods could be classified as Italian enclaves than could be classified as South Asian enclaves in 2001. Moreover, the insularity of Italian communities, what Hou calls the "within-group exposure index," was higher in 1981 than the analogous index among either the South Asian or Chinese populations of Toronto in 2001.

So why the panic now? South Asians and Chinese, being non-European, seem more obviously different from the majority. But in their day, Italians too (and Irish and Scottish and Poles, and the list goes on) were seen as worryingly different. When I was a teenager growing up in the Toronto suburb of Rexdale, the neighbourhood children of Italian immigrants, who spoke perfect English and shared my skin colour and even my religion, might as well have been from another planet. Kids my age, trumpeting their British or Italian or Irish roots, traded epithets and got into fist fights over differences that would soon come to seem microscopic. Most young people in Canada today are vastly more sophisticated than we were.

It's tempting to look back at earlier immigrants and imagine that we always knew it would work out. That we knew all along that these newcomers would make wonderful contributions to Canadian society, that their work, ideas, art, food, and, perhaps most of all, their children would make Canada better than it had been before. Concerns about immigration today are often accompanied by the claim that previous waves of immigrants weren't a worry because they came largely from the same (European, Christian) civilization as the British and French "founding nations." The story goes that today's newcomers, largely from Africa and Asia and thus from markedly different religious and cultural traditions, will have more trouble participating fully in the economic, political, and social life of Canada.

But European Christian immigrants excited plenty of worry in previous generations of Canadians when they arrived at this country's shores. Their successful integration into Canadian society was by no means a foregone conclusion. As Will Kymlicka astutely points out, some of the same concerns raised about Muslim immigrants today were raised a century ago about Catholics:

Catholics were perceived as undemocratic and unpatri-
otic because their allegiance was to the Pope, and as separatist because they demanded their own schools. The fear
that Catholics would not integrate took many years to
disappear; yet today they are seen as a vital component of
the mainstream society into which Muslims are allegedly
not integrating.[9]

The idea that "we" have successfully welcomed immigrants
in the past but that these *new* immigrants will be impossible
for the body politic (or economic or social) to digest isn't new.
"We" have thought this for a long time. The trick is that the
"we" isn't a stable group—it changes over time, expanding to
include each new wave of supposedly impossible-to-integrate
newcomers. Anxiety over the concentration of ethnic groups in
particular neighbourhoods is just one manifestation of the
perennial fear that the most recent set of new arrivals will be
the one that finally shatters the mosaic.

Still, even if it's not the case that Canadian cities are becoming increasingly balkanized along ethnic lines, it's worth exam-
ining what the socio-economic picture looks like in areas of
visible minority concentration. If these neighbourhoods are
characterized to some extent by poverty, that would be
evidence that Canada's diverse cities are beset with some perni-
cious problems.

A major study by two respected University of Toronto geographers tackles the question of the relationship between poverty and neighbourhood concentrations of visible minority groups.[10] Studying census data from 1991 and 2001, Alan Walks and Larry Bourne find that although these groups as a whole seem to be growing more concentrated, individual ethnic groups are not. In other words, while many neighbourhoods have growing visible minority populations, these populations tend to be internally diverse, containing members of any number of groups: Chinese, Southeast Asian, South Asian, black, Filipino, Latin American, Arab, Aboriginal, and so on. It is *not* the case that particular ethnic groups are becoming isolated and marginalized in poor, homogeneous neighbourhoods.

This is not to say that visible minorities don't face discrimination and other obstacles. In many cases neighbourhoods with high concentrations of visible minority residents are poorer than average. But Walks and Bourne find that racial concentration is far from the best predictor of neighbourhood poverty. More salient are, in order of importance, (a) high concentrations of apartment housing, (b) individual minority group proportions (some groups are consistently poorer), and (c) proportions of recent immigrants. In other words, balkanization along ethnic lines isn't leading to the isolation and impoverishment of visible minority groups in Canada. Indeed, some minority groups that are the least residentially concentrated, such as blacks, Aboriginals, and Latin Americans, have the greatest economic struggles while some of those that tend to be more concentrated, such as Chinese, South Asians, Jews, and Italians, experience notable success.

Some commentators have noted that increased economic inequality in Canada overall explains some of the difficulty experienced by some members of visible minority groups: as the rich become richer and the poor grow poorer, economic cleavages operate *within* ethnic groups. So it's not merely a case of whites becoming more affluent while visible minorities fall behind as a result of discrimination. The picture is more complicated: some South Asian Canadians are becoming more affluent while others remain static or get poorer. Some Chinese Canadians are getting richer while others are not. And so on for most groups.

The polarization of income and wealth in Western countries (and even rapidly developing countries like India and China) is a ubiquitous issue associated with economic globalization. It is not unfolding exclusively along racial lines, it is not limited to Canada, and it certainly has nothing to do with Canadian multiculturalism. Moreover, as University of Illinois at Chicago professor Walter Benn Michaels points out in his book *The Trouble with Diversity,* the emphasis on race instead of class can sometimes serve as a red herring in discussions of equality because people are often more comfortable celebrating cultural diversity than addressing economic inequality: "Diversity only asks us to give up our prejudices, equality asks us to give up our money."[11]

It's also worth noting that some visible minority groups are doing markedly better than others. Even among newcomer groups, some catch up to Canadian earning and employment averages more rapidly than others. It's not enough to say that visible minority Canadians aren't doing as well; there is too much diversity and too much complexity among them for such simplistic assessments to be of much use. This kind of analysis might work for some areas of the United States, where visible minority populations are often overwhelmingly black or Latin American, but in Canada the fact that a person isn't white tells us almost nothing.

The following charts are based on countries of origin. Not all Canadians who belong to visible minority groups are foreign-born, of course (Halifax's black community and Vancouver's Chinese community, to name only two, go back well beyond the earliest days of the Canadian state). Still, since most of Canada's visible minority citizens were born outside the country, looking at their nations of origin gives us a remarkable portrait not only of their geographic origins but of the ethnic diversity in our cities.

Proportions of Foreign-Born

City, Country	Total Foreign-born Population	Year
Dubai, United Arab Emirates	82%	2002
Miami, USA	51%	2000
Toronto, Canada	45%	2001
Muscat, Oman	45%	2000
Vancouver, Canada	39%	2001
Los Angeles, USA	36%	2000
New York, USA	34%	2000
Melbourne, Australia	29%	2001
London, UK	27%	2001

SOURCE: ADAPTED FROM "GLOBALIZATION FROM BELOW" BY LISA BENTON-SHORT/MARIE D. PRICE, AND SAMANTHA FRIEDMAN, IN *INTERNATIONAL JOURNAL OF URBAN AND REGIONAL RESEARCH*, VOL. 29.4, DECEMBER 2005

So much of the rhetoric about immigrant settlement in Western countries seems to assume that all immigrant populations are the same and that the challenges host countries face in integrating newcomers are the same. In fact, Canada's newcomers are markedly different from newcomers to countries like France, Britain, and the Netherlands for reasons ranging from colonial histories to immigration policies to simple geography. Some might look at the diversity under the

Nations of Origin of Immigrant Groups Comprising More than 1 Percent of Each City's Population

Toronto (14)*	Miami (9)	Vancouver (8)*	New York (8)
China	Cuba	China	Dominican Republic
India	Haiti	UK	China
UK	Colombia	India	Jamaica
Italy	Jamaica	Philippines	Mexico
Philippines	Nicaragua	Taiwan	Guyana
Jamaica	Venezuela	USA	Ecuador
Portugal	Peru	Vietnam	Haiti
Poland	Dominican Republic	South Korea	Colombia
Sri Lanka	Honduras		
Guyana			
Former USSR			
Vietnam			
Pakistan			
Former Yugoslavia			

*For Canadian cities, the unit of measurement is Census Metropolitan Area.

SOURCE: VARIOUS NATIONAL STATISTICS BUREAUS, VIA THE GLOBALIZATION URBANIZATION MIGRATION PROJECT, GEORGE WASHINGTON UNIVERSITY, HTTP://GSTUDYNET.ORG/GUM/INDEX.PHP?ABOUT

Los Angeles (7)	Melbourne (6)	Dubai (6)	Amsterdam (5)	London (4)
Mexico	UK	India	Suriname	India
El Salvador	Italy	Pakistan	Morocco	Ireland
Philippines	Vietnam	Various Arab	Turkey	Bangladesh
Guatemala	Greece	Bangladesh	Indonesia	Jamaica
South Korea	China	Philippines	Aruba and Netherlands Antilles	
China	New Zealand	Sri Lanka		
Vietnam				

Canadian headings in the chart above and imagine that it poses a greater challenge than for those cities with shorter lists. In fact, diversity seems to work better the more there is of it. As American society has shown us, a society with only two major racial groups—one affluent, the other persistently much less so—is anything but easy to manage. In Canadian society, although we have a long way to go, the sheer scale of our diversity may come to offset issues of prejudice and discrimination—or as one commentator put it, we may one day simply have too many races for racism to survive.

ECONOMIC OUTCOMES

Consider how difficult it is to migrate somewhere: the uprooting of a life and family, the severing of professional ties, the abandonment of familiar foods and landscapes and slants of light, the bureaucratic hassles, the struggle to understand and be understood, the sheer starting from scratch. In order to undertake such a monumental upheaval, people tend to need pretty substantial incentives. For some, it's the flight from violence or political persecution. Those familiar street corners are a lot less pleasing when you're worried you might be dragged off one of them to an unknown fate. But the incentive for most newcomers is the promise of economic opportunity—and by now it's no secret that Canada isn't always successful in delivering on that promise.

The Statistics Canada study of new immigrants (those who had arrived in the previous four years) released in spring 2007 reported some disheartening results.[12] Among economic-class immigrants—those whom Canada is trying most aggressively to attract in order to fuel innovation and economic growth— just a third (35 percent) said that their material circumstances were better now than before they immigrated. The majority said their material circumstances were the same as (31 percent) or *worse than* (34 percent) they were before they immigrated. Family-class immigrants (individuals who are admitted in order to be reunited with spouses, parents, or children) and refugees experienced higher levels of satisfaction with their material circumstances in Canada; majorities in both groups said they were better off financially in Canada than in their nations of origin. Still, it's the highly educated professionals in the economic category that are the central focus of Canada's current immigration project, and these people are clearly not experiencing the economic rewards they had anticipated.

Over the past couple of decades Canada has placed increasing emphasis on bringing in highly educated immigrants who can help drive a knowledge-based economy. Between 1992 and 2004 the proportion of newcomers falling into the "skilled worker" category grew from 29 percent to 51 percent—with concomitant declines in family-class immigrants and refugees. Whereas in 1992 just 17 percent of newcomers to Canada had university degrees, by 2004 that proportion had risen to 45 percent. (By comparison, just 23 percent of the total Canadian population hold university degrees.)

But while newcomers to Canada have become better educated, the incomes they earn when they arrive haven't improved. Although newcomers are on average better educated than the Canadian-born, their incomes lag behind the native-born considerably. Moreover, even in our globalized world full of supposedly mobile talent and transferable skills, there is evidence to suggest that the lot of immigrants to Canada has actually gotten worse over time.

Garnett Picot, Feng Hou, and Simon Coulombe of Statistics Canada use Statscan data to show that as of 2004, new Canadians were over three times as likely as the Canadian-born to have low incomes.[13] If you think that's not so bad— that these new Canadians are just finding their feet and will catch up soon enough—consider that even after ten years in Canada the foreign-born are more than twice as likely as the national average to have low incomes.

In time, the foreign-born do gain ground economically. But in addition to persistent inequality between newcomers and others, racial effects are evident in this area: white immigrants gain ground against the national average faster than racial minority immigrants do. Even setting migration status aside, it's clear that non-white Canadians face barriers that white Canadians don't. Jeffrey Reitz, a sociologist at the University of Toronto, and Rupa Banerjee, a PhD candidate at the school's Centre for Industrial Relations and Human Resources, use census data to point out that when Canadians' incomes are compared with average earnings in the cities where they live, visible minorities fall nearly $8000 below the local average while whites exceed the same average by nearly $2000.[14] This puts the total average gap between whites and non-whites at nearly $10,000 annually. Not very utopian.

Many reasons have been suggested as to why newcomers struggle economically—and continue to do so despite high levels of skill and education. For one thing, as Canada's economy is ever more information- and service-oriented, language skills become increasingly important. A newcomer could arrive in the 1950s with no English and be laying bricks or installing drywall the next day. Today, full participation in an economy that relies so heavily on verbal and written communication skills requires very high levels of competence in one or both of Canada's official languages; for some newcomers, perfecting these skills will take time. Even an accent can be a barrier.

Similarly, as skills become less tangible, paper qualifications become ever more important. Hire a carpenter and you can probably tell by the end of the day whether she's ever done the job before. But hire an MBA and things are less clear-cut. As a result, employers tend to care a great deal about which institution granted that MBA (or law, medical, or engineering degree). If the institution is unfamiliar because it's halfway around the world, the disadvantage to its bearer may be unspoken but powerful.

Of course, there's also old-fashioned discrimination. This is difficult to quantify, particularly in a climate where overt bigotry is socially unacceptable. But when a 23 percent earnings gap prevails between whites and non-whites, it's hard to deny that something smells rotten.

There are some signs of improvement, however. Peter S. Li, a sociologist at the University of Saskatchewan, finds that, although immigrants' situations upon arrival in Canada have gotten worse since the early 1990s, the rate at which newcomers gain ground against the Canadian average is increasing over time.[15]

In addition, the need for better newcomer employment outcomes, recognition of foreign paper qualifications, and vigilance about discrimination are all issues that are rising higher on the public agenda. The last two federal budgets have included investments specifically intended to improve new immigrants' labour market outcomes. As well, a new Foreign Credentials Referral Office has been established to help smooth the entry of people with foreign paper qualifications into the Canadian workforce. Organizations like the Toronto Region Immigrant Employment Council (TRIEC) and Vancouver's S.U.C.C.E.S.S. are undertaking strategic projects—such as mentoring and networking programs for newcomer professionals—to help build up the human connections that are so often the starting points for new careers. Economically, immigrants and Canada aren't currently getting the best from each other. But there is much evidence that Canadian leaders are paying attention and working to make things better.

Another hopeful sign is the employment outcomes of second-generation Canadians: the children of immigrants. Looking at the average incomes of three groups—those whose families have been in Canada for three generations or more, immigrants, and children of immigrants—it is the last group, the second generation, that has the highest earnings. According to Statistics Canada, second-generation Canadian men earn an average annual income of about $49,000, as compared with about $42,000 for those whose families have been here three or more generations.[16] Second-generation women earn an average income of about $32,000 as compared with about $27,000 for those whose families have been here longer. These numbers suggest that for many immigrant families in Canada, the storied dream of starting over in a foreign country to make life better for their children is coming true.

Although good employment outcomes are crucial indicators of newcomer success and the fairness of the society that welcomes them, it bears noting that personal income isn't everything. It's true that only a third of economic-class immigrants say their material circumstances are better now than prior to their migration. But fully 84 percent say their overall quality of life is better. This may well be a measure of our rich public domain: urban libraries are doing a tremendous job of reaching out to newcomers, and Canadian parks, schools, health care, and other public services are by no means trivial influences on quality of life for Canadians new and old. Satisfaction with quality of life in Canada is even higher among refugees and family-class immigrants. Moreover, the Statistics Canada report on recent immigrants indicates that when newcomers are asked what they like *least* about Canada, the most common answer (26.7 percent) is the weather. The second most common answer is *nothing* (19 percent). In third place—and the first thing on the list that Canadians can actually do something about, other than trying to speed up global warming to keep our newcomers from more temperate climates cozy—is the lack of employment opportunities (17.4 percent). This is not to diminish the urgency of the issue; doing the work that one is capable of and being appropriately rewarded are extremely important to all of us. But as we strive for better immigrant employment outcomes, it's worth remembering that the vast majority of newcomers to Canada love the country, are happy with—and would repeat!—their decision to come here, and that there are resources of considerable energy and goodwill on all sides in the effort to make sure that Canada and its newest citizens get the best from each other.

POLITICAL REPRESENTATION

Some of the most significant indicators of how newcomers are faring in their adoptive country relate to their level of political engagement, which includes things like taking out citizenship (Canada is outstanding in the extent to which newcomers seek citizenship) and voting. An especially powerful form of participation is running for—and winning—political office. Of course, when we talk about the people involved in public life we're talking about only a tiny sliver of society; the House of Commons, after all, has just 308 seats. Still, we tend to believe that the composition of elected legislatures says something about the broader social conditions in the countries they govern. We tend to think, for example, that if groups not traditionally well represented in politics—women, racial minorities, people with disabilities, and so on—begin to gain office, it's not only a good thing in itself but also an indication of more widespread social progress: the determination and ability of minority groups to marshal the considerable resources necessary to mount a political campaign, and the willingness of the electorate to vote for them.

When it comes to newcomers to Canada, the level of political participation is remarkable. For one thing, if you're paying any attention at all to politics, it probably means you're not being forced to focus exclusively on the basic necessities of life. Only when people have taken care of the essentials—food, shelter, clothing—are they able to pause and think about such abstract issues as taxes, social programs, law and order, foreign policy, and other collective priorities. Certainly you might see political involvement as a way to improve the circumstances of immigrants or refugees, but if you're having trouble feeding your family or paying the rent, getting your name on a ballot is hardly the most direct route to solving that problem.

Beyond the basic material stability that political engagement tends to signify, newcomers' (or indeed anyone's) participation in politics suggests other hopeful signs. People arriving in Canada evidently think politics is an effective way of participating in—and changing—the workings of their adoptive country. If the political system were seen as hopelessly corrupt or ineffective, there wouldn't be much reason to become involved. Moreover, if newcomers saw the electorate as so racist or xenophobic that someone born outside the country or having a minority ethnocultural background stood no chance of being elected, these new Canadians would stay home.

The flip side of that faith in the electorate, of course, is the electorate itself. When immigrants are elected, it suggests that voters believe they're competent, that they understand the issues, that they're able to effectively represent their constituents' concerns in a legislative setting, and that they've taken the goals and values of the country sufficiently to heart that they'll make valuable contributions to national governance. Those who vote for the foreign-born are saying that new Canadians are just as qualified to represent their communities as anyone whose family has been here for generations.

In other words, if immigrants are in Parliament, something is working—and working well. In Canada, immigrants are in Parliament. In fact, Canada has the highest proportion of foreign-born legislators in the world. This is true in two ways. First, we have the world's largest proportion of seats in our lower legislative chamber (the House of Commons) occupied by people who weren't born here. Second, our proportion of foreign-born legislators comes the closest in the world to matching the proportion of foreign-born people in the country's population overall.

According to the 2001 census, 19.3 percent of Canadians were born outside Canada. And as of April 2007, 13 percent of the members of Parliament at the federal level were born outside Canada. This is not perfect parity; the ratio of foreign-born legislators to foreign-born Canadians is about 2 to 3. But Canada is doing the best job in the world when it comes to matching its elected legislative body with the people who actually live in the country. And remember: not all of our foreign-born are yet citizens who are able to vote and seek public office.

In Australia—again, often seen as Canada's twin on matters of immigration and multiculturalism—the proportion of foreign-born legislators to foreign-born Australians is less than half: 11 percent of Australia's House of Representatives is made up of people born outside Australia, while 23 percent of Australia's population is foreign-born.

In Great Britain, 7.5 percent of the population is foreign-born. Of the 646 seats in the British House of Commons, 29 are occupied by foreign-born members, putting foreign-born representation at about 4.5 percent. If the British House reflected the British population perfectly, it would contain forty-eight foreign-born MPs, including eight from Africa (there are currently four), sixteen from Asia (there are currently seven), and twenty-one from elsewhere in Europe (there are currently four).

In France, where 10.6 percent of the population is foreign-born, 6.2 percent of deputies in the National Assembly were born outside the country. If one looks at the places of birth of these foreign-born legislators, they appear to hail mostly from African nations formerly colonized by France: Tunisia,

Morocco, and Algeria. A look at the faces and names of these legislators suggests that they're largely the children of French diplomats and bureaucrats—not people whose ancestors are from North Africa. Deputies Dupont, Besson, Deniaud, Lellouche, Le Fur, and Paix are all African-born. So, of course, is the famous Ségolène Royale, born in Senegal but so passionate about her adoptive (and ancestral!) country that one plank of her presidential platform was that every home should contain a tricolour flag and every person should be capable of belting out France's national anthem, "La Marseillaise." These African-born deputies may be very fine legislators and likely bring a special perspective to their jobs, but they don't attest to the potential for immigrants of North African origin—with non-white faces and non-French names—to attain the highest rungs of French public life. If we look at the number of Asian deputies in the National Assembly (zero deputies, when parity with the population would suggest four) or those from elsewhere in Europe (seven deputies, when parity would suggest twenty-six) we may get a clearer picture of the chances of the foreign-born attaining French political office.

In the United States the disparity between residents is especially large: just 2 percent of the House of Representatives were born outside the country, while as of 2006 the American population was 14.7 percent foreign-born. The famous American melting pot has yet to melt many immigrants into

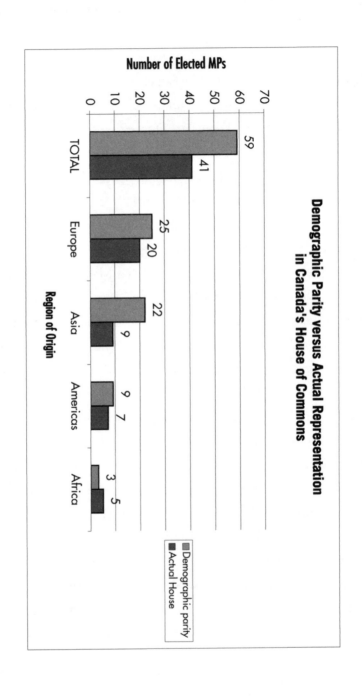

Demographic Parity versus Actual Representation in Canada's House of Commons

Number of Elected MPs

Region of Origin

TOTAL — 59, 41
Europe — 25, 20
Asia — 22, 9
Americas — 9, 7
Africa — 3, 5

Demographic parity
Actual House

Congress. Some might argue, however, that California's gubernator, Austrian-born movie star Arnold Schwarzenegger, makes up for this lack of foreign-born political representation in sheer muscular charisma.

When we look at the nations of origin of various Western countries' foreign-born legislators, we find that Canada's lower house is once again the closest to being representative of the overall population. If, mirroring the country itself, 19 percent of the House of Commons were made up of foreign-born MPs, then we'd have fifty-nine foreign-born MPs. Twenty-five of these would be from Europe, twenty-two from Asia, nine from the Americas, and three from Africa. In fact, we have forty-one foreign-born MPs. Twenty of these are from Europe, nine from Asia, seven from the Americas (three from Latin America, two from the Caribbean, two from the United States), and five from Africa. Although Asian-born Canadians are notably underrepresented in the House, the proportions of MPs born in Africa, the Americas, and Europe come fairly close to matching—or in the case of Africa actually exceed— the proportions of the Canadian population born in those regions.

Australia is second to Canada in terms of the sheer number of foreign-born members of the lower house. But Australia's House looks less like Australia than Canada's House looks like Canada. Of 150 members of the Australian

House of Representatives, fifteen are foreign-born. Of these fifteen, eleven are European. While 6.4 percent of Australia's population was born in Asia (suggesting that a perfectly demographically representative House would have ten Asian-born MPs), just one Australian representative was born in Asia.

As the graphic on the facing page shows, the United States, France, and Great Britain are even further from fully representing their foreign-born population in their lower legislative houses.

The point of this discussion isn't merely to boast. In many ways, the House of Commons isn't completely representative of the Canadian population, and this applies not just to the foreign-born but to visible minorities, women, and other traditionally underrepresented groups. Still, Canada is leading the pack in the election of legislators born outside the country—and is thus fostering a legislative body aligned with the makeup of the population at large.

Naturally, people are individuals—not just collections of demographic traits. Some of our foreign-born MPs will help give voice to their own ethnocultural communities while at the same time serving their diverse constituencies. (Or so we always hope, wherever we're from and however long we've lived here.) Others will govern without much regard to their nation of origin or their compatriots from outside Canada.

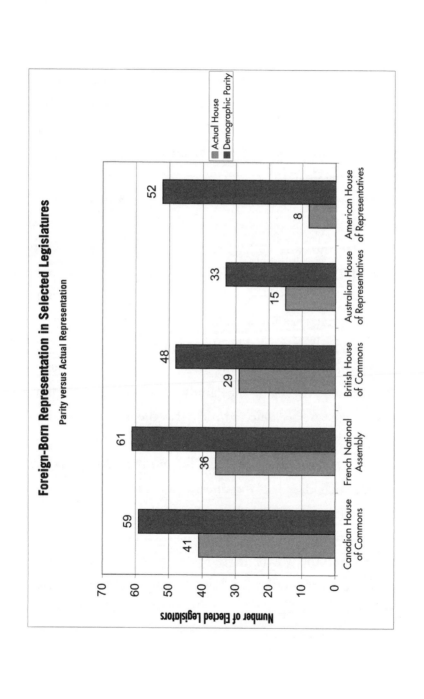

Foreign-Born Representation in Selected Legislatures

Parity versus Actual Representation

Number of Elected Legislators

- Actual House
- Demographic Parity

Canadian House of Commons: 59, 41
French National Assembly: 61, 36
British House of Commons: 48, 29
Australian House of Representatives: 33, 15
American House of Representatives: 52, 8

Moreover, the more than three dozen foreign-born MPs in the House of Commons represent every major political party in this country, from the Conservatives to the Bloc Québécois. In many European countries it's unthinkable that an immigrant would join the most conservative party in the system, since the most conservative parties tend also to be the most xenophobic; Canada's Conservatives, however, are (officially) as positive about immigration as any other party. (In the early 1990s Preston Manning's Reform Party called for a decrease in immigration rates but subsequently had to revise its platform in the face of public backlash.) And the fact that foreign-born citizens would run for the Bloc is equally remarkable. What better sign of integration could there be than immigrants' feeling so at home in Canada that they join the family feud? (Do many immigrants join and seek elected office for the Scottish National Party or Spain's Catalan independentist party, ERC?)

But whatever political views foreign-born MPs espouse, the fact that they had the interest and the resources to run and the fact that their ridings elected them can signify only success: success for the MPs in their adoptive country, and success for the voters in their local communities who've chosen the person they think is the best candidate regardless of his or her background.

But not so fast.

Canadians, a perpetually fretful bunch, aren't so easily convinced. The fact that we have so many foreign-born MPs may actually be a bad sign, I've been told. And not by xenophobes who don't wish to see immigrants in Parliament, but rather by well-intentioned people who worry that Canada just cannot get this multiculturalism thing right. They tell me that our forty-one foreign-born MPs merely offer more evidence of those nasty ethnic enclaves; that newcomers and minority groups are segregating themselves into highly concentrated neighbourhoods and electing members of their own tribes— while Canadian-born people of British or French extraction hunker down in their own enclaves and do the same. In this analysis, foreign-born MPs don't signify successful integration and non-discriminatory voting, but quite the opposite: electoral ghettoization.

Analysis of these MPs' ridings suggests that this is not the case. Foreign-born Canadians who have run for and won elected office in this country have for the most part been elected by diverse ridings—and in some cases ridings that *do* have a dominant ethnic group, but one that doesn't match the MP's own. It's good news, I'm afraid. I hope Canadians won't take it too hard.

Using data from our geodemographic practice, Environics Analytics, we looked at the ethnic and immigrant composition of ridings where the forty-one foreign-born MPs were elected in the January 2006 federal election. And it's true that some of these MPs were elected in ridings with high concentrations of people of their own national or ethnocultural background. For example, Maurizio Bevilacqua, the Italian-born MP for the Ontario riding of Vaughan, was elected in a riding that's 56 percent ethnically Italian.[17] Moreover, over one in five residents of Vaughan (21.4 percent) were, like Bevilacqua, born in Italy. Similarly, Raymond Chan, the Hong Kong–born MP for the B.C. riding of Richmond South Delta, was elected by a group of Canadians who are 42 percent ethnically Chinese. In Chan's riding, more than half of the population is foreign-born (58 percent), and nearly three in ten were born in either Hong Kong (17 percent) or mainland China (12 percent). But Vaughan and Richmond South Delta are the exceptions, not the rule. Of all the ridings in Canada that elected foreign-born MPs in the last election, these two have the highest concentrations of voters whose backgrounds match that of the elected MP.[18] Most of the other forty-one ridings with foreign-born MPs are instances of one of two other scenarios.

The first scenario is that the riding has a moderate concentration of voters who share the MP's background. In Ontario's Bramalea-Gore-Malton, for example, which elected Indian-born Gurbax Malhi, about 18 percent are ethnically Indian and 13 percent were born in India. But even if every one of these Indian-identified residents had voted and voted for Malhi, 18 percent would not have been enough to elect him; he must have done something to appeal to the residents of his riding who identify their background as Italian (7.5 percent), Jamaican (4.8 percent), Guyanese (1.1 percent), Filipino (1.7 percent), or English (4.4 percent). He might also have struck a chord with the one in ten who simply call themselves Canadian and, wherever they're from, identify with none of the ethnic groups listed.

The second scenario is that the MP's nation of origin seems to have almost no correlation at all with the riding. Take Jim Karygiannis, the Greek-born MP elected in the Greater Toronto riding of Scarborough-Agincourt. Karygiannis's riding is 35.7 percent ethnically Chinese, with about a quarter of the population born in either Hong Kong (11 percent) or mainland China (15 percent). Just 3 percent of the residents of Scarborough-Agincourt are Greek. In other words, the citizens of what some might define as a Chinese "ethnic enclave" sent a Greek-born Canadian to Ottawa to represent them in the federal legislative body. Is it possible that Canadians of different backgrounds are talking to each other, and finding that the conversation actually makes sense? That in matters of health policy or child care or taxes or education, your Greek neighbour might be speaking your language after all?

Politics is only one (relatively small) part of our lives as Canadians. It is rare indeed that people consider politics or citizenship to be more important than family, work, play, or the neighbourhood they live in. For many Canadians, it doesn't much matter who sits in Parliament—and many of us would say that our MP doesn't represent us in any way that feels very meaningful. That said, the government still runs the country. *Someone* is going to sit in Ottawa and make decisions that—whether we take much personal notice or not—affect us all. I believe it's a very good sign that people can come to this country as children or as adults and not only deem our institutions sufficiently relevant to merit involvement but actually run and be elected. We live in a country in which newcomers have the confidence and resources to run for office, the social networks that can connect them to our federal political parties, and the willingness (and optimism) to participate in our democracy. And we live in a country where their fellow Canadians—of whatever background—will vote for them.

Our system may not be perfect. But those who claim that the whole thing is hopelessly dysfunctional had better have a good answer to Jim Karygiannis, his Chinese electors, and the forty other immigrant MPs who represent their diverse constituents in some of the highest offices in the country.

INTERMARRIAGE (SEX IN THE SNOW?)

The final frontier.

Whenever different kinds of people live side by side, the question arises of just how much they should interact. Should you do business with the other? (Can she or he be trusted?) Should you live next door to the other? Should your kids go to school together? Of course, once people start interacting to any serious degree, friendships are almost inevitable and someone at some point might just fall in love. Literature is full of the story—so perfectly individual in the lovers' minds—of romantic love constrained by social cleavages, usually of tribe or class. But if people don't meet, or meet only superficially, they're unlikely to have a chance to fall in love in the first place. Or if people live in a society where prejudice is especially obdurate, even if they do fall in love they may be unable to overcome social disapproval of their taboo union. It follows that if Canadian multiculturalism were, as alleged, leading to a society riven by ethnic separation, one would expect rates of intermarriage to be declining. People of different backgrounds would be meeting less, and if they did meet, it would be in a state of wariness and mutual ignorance not conducive to social, let alone romantic, intimacy.

But intermarriage is increasing in Canada. As of 2001, of the roughly fourteen million Canadians in couples (either marriages or common-law unions), over 450,000 individuals were in mixed unions.[19] (Mixed unions are defined by Statistics Canada as a union between either a visible minority individual and a non-visible minority individual, or two visible minority individuals of different backgrounds.) Although Canadians in mixed unions remain a fairly small minority (about 3 percent), their numbers increased by 35 percent between 1991 and 2001. In general, mixed unions can be expected to lead to more mixed unions: as one mixed couple knits together their respective networks of friends and family, interactions across ethnic groups increase. And as any speed-dating coordinator will tell you, sometimes it doesn't take much interaction to spark a lasting connection.

Proportions of Canadian Couples in Mixed Unions

Age	1991	2001
15–19	4	5.4
20–29	4	5.3
30–39	3.4	4.8
40–49	2.8	3.2
50+	1.3	1.8

SOURCE: STATISTICS CANADA, CENSUS

Another reason why we might expect mixed marriages to continue to increase is that young people seem to like them more than older people do. Young people are harbingers of the future, and are frequently more open to difference than are their elders. Whereas the proportion of Canadians over the age of fifty in mixed couples is 1.8 percent, the corresponding proportion of those aged twenty to twenty-nine is 5.3 percent. In other words, young Canadians today are three times as likely as their parents to be in mixed unions.

People with higher levels of education are also more likely to be in mixed unions. Among university-educated Canadians, 5.6 percent are mated to someone outside their ethnic group, as compared with 1.5 percent of those with less than a high school diploma. And if high levels of education help to open people's minds and social circles, then as Canadian society (including newcomers) becomes ever more highly educated we can expect to see a growing number of mixed unions in this country.

Not surprisingly, intermarriage is most common in Canadian cities, which are home to the most diverse populations. Vancouver has the highest proportion of mixed unions in the country, followed by Toronto. And when you put young people (natural mixers) in cities (natural mixing places), mixed unions become even more common: among Vancouverites in their twenties who have paired off, 13 percent are with a partner who is not of their own background. (In Toronto the number is 11 percent, in Montreal 6 percent.) That means one in eight young Vancouverites is sharing ideas, friends, food, a home, a bed, in-laws, and perhaps children with someone their parents or grandparents could never have imagined.

Rates of intermarriage vary markedly across groups, and in some cases are surprisingly high. Japanese Canadians are the most likely to intermarry; 70 percent of those who are in couples are with a non-Japanese partner. Intermarriage rates are also high among Latin Americans (45 percent), blacks (43 percent), and Filipinos (33 percent). They are lower, but not trivial, among South Asian (13 percent) and Chinese (16 percent) Canadians.

The rates of intermarriage in this country point to an evolution that goes far beyond grudging mutual acceptance. As a society, Canadians have moved from merely tolerating difference to accommodating, savouring, and exploring it. Young people, of course, are at the forefront of this evolution. Experimental by nature, and often fascinated by the trappings of identity—clothing, music, makeup, postures—they like to try things on. Some things fit, others don't. But the willingness to try—to be immersed, for example, in a large family with unfamiliar rituals and expectations—is one of the great flexibilities of the young. The inclination to defy convention, brave elders' raised eyebrows, and insist on pursuing the relationship one finds most personally satisfying is another attribute that seems to reside disproportionately among the young. But young or old, rates of intermarriage are increasing rapidly, and the religious buildings and banquet halls of the nation are being filled with a small but growing number of Big Fat Canadian Weddings.

If Canada is becoming a hopelessly segregated society, rising rates of intermarriage are a strange symptom of the alleged disease.

three

Muslims in Canada

FATHER, SHOCKED AT DAUGHTER'S ATTIRE:
You look like a Protestant.
DAUGHTER: *Dad, you mean a prostitute.*
FATHER: *No, I mean a Protestant.*
—CBC's *Little Mosque on the Prairie*

If a martian had arrived in Canada in spring 2007 he might have been confused by the media coverage of a few high-profile controversies over head scarves worn by some Muslim women. There was the young soccer player ejected from a tournament because her hijab was declared dangerous attire by the referee (himself a Muslim). There was a young woman newly employed by a Quebec correctional facility who was told that if she wanted to keep coming to work she'd have to appear without her hijab. (She stayed home.) There were the women in niqabs (head coverings that conceal the face) voting in the Quebec provincial election: if their identity couldn't be verified with photo ID, should they be permitted to cast ballots? The chief electoral officer, reversing his original decision when it was met with a storm of controversy, declared that niqab-wearing women would have to show their faces in order to vote.

The visiting Martian might have been baffled by all this talk about religious headgear because it would have been plain to him, had he done any research at all, that such attire is hardly unheard of in Canada. Our Supreme Court decided years ago that Sikh Mounties, on grounds of religious freedom, had the right to wear their turbans rather than the traditional Stetsons of the RCMP. Any inhabitant of Canada's major cities sees plenty of other religious attire: yarmulkes worn by observant Jews, crosses worn by Christians, and, on occasion, the wimples that were a familiar sight to me as a Catholic boy educated by nuns. (To those who see no danger in such familiar Christian religious costumes, I assure you from personal experience: a habit can conceal a sizeable strap, which can be extricated from that flowing gown and deployed against an insolent hand with terrifying swiftness.)

So why all the fuss about the various coverings (the hijab, niqab, and chador) worn by a minority of Muslim women in Canada? (Our Environics survey found that just 42 percent of Canadian Muslim women wear a head scarf of any kind. Of these, almost all wear a hijab, which covers the hair but leaves the entire face exposed to neighbours, colleagues, and Quebec electoral officials. Only 3 percent wear a niqab, which covers everything except the eyes.) I believe there are two reasons for the alarm some Canadians express about these garments. First is the concern about gender inequality: the idea that Muslim head scarves symbolize the subordination of women to men according to traditional religious laws. Second is the concern that head scarves signify an embrace of religious codes at the expense of full participation in secular Canadian life, a kind of willful separation of their wearers from the wider society.

The question of gender equality is an interesting one (discussed more fully in the final chapter), but suffice it to say that in this time and place it's impossible to know people's reasons for wearing religious attire without hearing from them directly. Some hijabis (women who wear hijabs) might say that they wear them out of a sense of sexual modesty or deference to Muslim men. Others will say that Muslim men have nothing to do with it, that their wearing of the hijab is between them and God—a sign of deference to Allah, not to any man on this planet. Still others see their wearing of the hijab as a downright feminist gesture: an embrace of their identity as Muslim women and a sign of steadfastness in the face of whatever forces—within or outside the Muslim community— might seek to marginalize or dismiss them.

Readers interested in unpacking some of the possible meanings of young women wearing the hijab might wish to read Nobel Prize–winner Orhan Pamuk's wonderful novel *Snow*. One of its central characters, Kadife, dons a hijab for romantic purposes: to gain the affections of a charismatic and devout Muslim militant. And readers of Ariel Levy's wryly hilarious

Female Chauvinist Pigs: Women and the Rise of Raunch Culture
may come away from *that* book wondering whether a hijab
isn't preferable to (and indeed more feminist than) some of the
hypersexual getups that pass for uniforms of sexual empower-
ment in contemporary America. Sex and power are always
complicated, however you dress them up—or undress them.

If we were to fret about all faiths with a tradition of gender
inequality, or wring our hands over every religious text that can
be read as relegating women to second-class status, we'd have a
lot more than Islam on our hands. Prominent political analyst
Janice Stein has written eloquently about her own struggles in
her synagogue, interpreting these as a kind of microcosm of
broader socio-political negotiations. With the exception of a
few First Nations traditions, every faith ever practised in
Canada is probably guilty of promoting gender inequality in
some form. When Canadians express worry about the hijab—
and no small number do: a third of all Canadians (36 percent)
say they think the banning of Muslim head scarves in public
places such as schools is a good idea, and in Quebec, whose
daughters were populating nunneries only a generation ago, a
slim majority (53 percent) think such a ban would be a good
idea—they are worrying about more than a perceived sartorial
expression of gender inequality.

It is the latter concern—about Muslim Canadians' willingness to participate fully in Canadian society—that is more

relevant to discussions of Canadian multiculturalism. When Quebecers debated whether it was acceptable for women to wear the niqab or the burqa to polling stations in the spring 2007 election, there was talk of "the limits of reasonable accommodation" and multiculturalism's being "a two-way street" (that is, a street on which minority groups had to make efforts to adapt to the wider society that in turn accommodated their differences). Clearly, the wearing of these face-obscuring scarves was seen as a flouting of some social code, even though provincial law *already* permitted any Quebecer to vote without showing their face (using a provision that allows a second party to attest to the identity of any voter, provided that second person shows photo identification). In other words, Quebec's lawmakers had already decided that the kind of situation raised by the niqab or burqa could be acceptable as long as another condition was met. But in the case of Muslim women there was some sense that the concealment of the face was an unacceptable violation of the rules—or at least of social mores. Many Quebecers—represented most bombastically by Action démocratique du Québec (ADQ) leader Mario Dumont, but certainly not chastised by the other leaders who appeared intimidated by the backlash Dumont was harnessing so successfully—seemed to feel that Muslims weren't meeting them halfway on that two-way street of multiculturalism.

Was all this fuss really about a handful of women wearing head scarves? (Estimates put the number of Quebec Muslim women who wear the niqab or burqa at less than a hundred.) Looking at the results of our surveys of Muslim Canadians and the population at large, it seems unlikely that the debate is actually about fabric and photo ID. More likely, it's about some Canadians' perception that some immigrants to this country do not approach their relationship with Canada's people, laws, and culture in good faith. When we ask a representative sample of Canadians whether they believe that most Muslims in this country wish to adopt Canadian customs and the Canadian way of life, or whether most Muslims wish to remain distinct from Canadian society at large, a majority of Canadians (57 percent) say they think Muslims want to remain distinct.

But when we ask Muslims themselves the same question, the majority (also 57 percent) say they believe most Muslims in Canada want to adopt Canadian customs. And an additional 13 percent say they think most Muslims wish to adopt Canadian customs *and* remain a distinct community. Combined, this means that seven in ten Canadian Muslims believe that their fellow Muslims are interested in integrating into the "Canadian way of life"—either while maintaining a distinct Muslim identity or not. Less than a quarter (23 percent) of Canadian Muslims believe that most of their coreligionists in this country want primarily to remain distinct from the wider society.

This was the first ever survey of the attitudes of Muslims in Canada, and it yielded many interesting results. (The precise wording of the questions cited in this chapter, and a description of the survey's methodology, can be found in the Appendix.) But this finding struck me as the most significant. The disjunction between how Muslims view their own desire to integrate and how other Canadians view it is pronounced: while Muslims see themselves as wanting to participate in and adapt to Canadian society (even as they sustain religious and ethnocultural ties as so many Canadians have always done and are encouraged to do), the population at large tends to doubt this willingness. If Canadians overall sensed that the vast majority of Muslims wished to integrate into social and economic life in their adopted country, would the question of women wearing hijabs or even niqabs be so charged? It seems unlikely. It is precisely the underlying anxiety about minority religious groups' willingness to integrate that infuses more superficial debates (such as those about clothing) with such passion and fear.

Skeptics may say, "So what? Even if Muslims think their coreligionists want to integrate into Canadian society, they may be wrong." But some of the other responses Muslim Canadians gave to our survey questions further illuminate their attitudes on these complex issues of identity.

The vast majority of Canadian Muslims (about nine in ten) were born outside Canada. Most Muslims, then, have come to this country from elsewhere and like most immigrants presumably have strong ties—both familial and emotional—to their birth countries. How strong is their attachment to Canada? Ninety-four percent say they're proud to be Canadian (matching the national average of 93 percent). Nearly three-quarters (73 percent) describe themselves as *very* proud. Moreover, among foreign-born Muslims, pride in being Canadian grows with time spent in the country. Among those who have lived in Canada fewer than five years, a solid majority of 73 percent describe themselves as proud, 54 percent very proud. (Twelve percent might be proud but tell us they're not yet Canadian citizens.) Among foreign-born Muslims who've been in Canada more than fifteen years, however, 99 percent say they're proud to be Canadian, with 88 percent proclaiming they are very proud.

When we ask Canadian Muslims what characteristics of this country make them proud to be Canadian, their answers mirror the responses of the population at large. Muslim Canadians tell us that they're proud of Canadian freedom and democracy, multiculturalism, the fact that Canada is a peaceful country, the idea that Canada is a caring and friendly country, and the fact that Canada is a safe place to live. When they're asked what they like *least* about life in this country, the most common answer, cited by a quarter of respondents, is the weather, a response that parallels the findings of Statistics Canada's Longitudinal Survey of Immigrants to Canada (cited earlier) conducted among all immigrant groups. Among Canadians at large, the weather is the second most often cited pitfall of life in this country, after the government. (Perhaps with more time in Canada, foreign-born Muslims will come to agree with the rest of the country that the government—any government—tends to be more depressing than the weather.)

Greatest Sources of Pride in Canada

Q. What is it about Canada that gives you the greatest source of pride?

Muslim Canadians	% citing	All Canadians	% citing
Freedom/democracy	33	Freedom/democracy	27
Multiculturalism	17	Multiculturalism	11
Peaceful country	10	Humanitarian/kind/caring	9
Humanitarian/caring/friendly	9	Peaceful country	6
Safe/low crime rate	4	Beauty of land/geography	4
Tolerance/respect/equality	3	Quality of life	3

SOURCES: ENVIRONICS SURVEY OF CANADIAN MUSLIMS, DECEMBER 2006, JANUARY 2007, FOCUS CANADA 2006

Looking at all these pride-inspiring factors together—freedom, peace, safety, multiculturalism—one might surmise that Muslim Canadians think Canada is a pretty good place to live. Their answers to our other questions suggest that they do. In their survey responses many express concerns about discrimination as well as unemployment and underemployment in the Muslim community. Still, in addition to their high levels of pride in Canada, Muslims tend to indicate that they feel they're living in a successful country where their overall quality of life is high.

Muslims also express the belief that Canada is on the right track as a country. Ninety-one percent say that overall they think Canada is headed in a good direction. On this measure they outscore the general population by twenty points: 71 percent of all Canadians say Canada's on the right track.

By and large, Canadian Muslims also seem pleased with their decision to immigrate to Canada rather than to another Western country. Nearly eight in ten (77 percent) say that Muslims are treated better in Canada than they are in other Western countries. Most of the rest (17 percent) say that Muslims are treated about the same here as elsewhere in the West. Just 3 percent believe that Muslims are worse off in Canada than they would be elsewhere in the West.

Of course, any minority group's lot in a country has a great deal to do with their fellow citizens. No small part of Muslim Canadians' sense that they're better off in this country has to do with how they see their fellow Canadians' attitudes toward them. Asked what proportion of Canadians are hostile toward Muslims, just 5 percent say that most Canadians are hostile. This is an interesting item because it encourages people to consider the overall atmosphere in the country—not just whether they themselves have experienced discrimination but the experiences of their families and friends and their sense of the general social climate. Fully three-quarters of Canadian Muslims say that "just some" (39 percent) or "very few" (35 percent) Canadians are hostile to people of their faith. As the graphic below shows, Canadian Muslims stand out on this question when compared with Muslims in Great Britain, Spain, Germany, and France. In all those countries, Muslims are more likely to sense greater hostility toward adherents of Islam.

Perceived Hostility toward Muslims

Q. In your opinion, how many Canadians/Europeans do you think are hostile to Muslims?
Would you say most, many, just some, or very few?
(proportions shown said "most" or "many")

	Canada	Great Britain	France	Spain	Germany
Muslims	17	42	39	31	51
General population	28	40	56	60	63

SOURCES: CANADIAN DATA ARE FROM ENVIRONICS; INTERNATIONAL DATA ARE FROM PEW GLOBAL ATTITUDES PROJECT, "MUSLIMS IN EUROPE," 6 JULY 2006

All this is not to say that Canadian Muslims don't experience discrimination or don't *see themselves* as experiencing discrimination. Many do, on both counts. Nearly one in three (31 percent) report that they've "had a bad experience" related to their race, ethnicity, or religion in the past two years. And Canada doesn't stand out much from European countries in this regard; only in France are Muslims more likely to report experiences of discrimination, while they're somewhat less likely to in Great Britain, Spain, and Germany. (Notably, Muslim women are more likely than men to report experiences of discrimination, which may be a symptom of the hijab's making Muslim women more readily identifiable to those inclined to discriminate.)

The issue of discrimination emerges elsewhere in our survey as well. To the question of what Canadian Muslims like least about Canada—where the top answer was the weather—the second most common answer was less amusing: discrimination. It was a top-of-mind concern about life in Canada for 13 percent of Canadian Muslims (as compared with 24 percent who were more worried about the arctic chill).

But the proportion of Muslims who express concern about discrimination is much higher than 13 percent. It's one thing to ask someone to name a drawback of life in Canada off the top of their head; it's another thing to ask about a slate of issues. When we ask Muslims about their level of concern regarding various matters, from discrimination to unemployment to the secularization of Muslim youth, discrimination is close to the top of the list: two-thirds of Canadian Muslims (66 percent) say they're concerned about discrimination against Muslims in this country, and three in ten (30 percent) say they're very concerned. Notably, concern about discrimination is higher among younger Muslims; this isn't surprising, since younger people are also more likely to say they've been discriminated against. There is some evidence to suggest that young people (especially second-generation Canadians) take discrimination more to heart than do their parents. Generally, adults who decide to immigrate to a new country expect to put up with a certain degree of hardship and prejudice; provided their lives are generally improving, they may be willing to overlook an epithet here or there. But their children, raised, educated, or even born in Canada (and steeped in the rhetoric of multiculturalism that holds everyone to be equal), are less likely to suffer discrimination without feeling considerable disappointment in their new society. They feel betrayed.

The only thing that concerns Canadian Muslims as much as discrimination is unemployment: two-thirds (65 percent) say they're worried about it; a third (33 percent) are very worried. And of course, discrimination and unemployment can't be completely disentangled. Since the Muslim population is so heavily foreign-born, the recognition of foreign credentials, language skills, and other employment issues linked to migration surely affect their employment fortunes. Although such barriers may not be seen as discrimination in its purest form—that is, the conscious refusal to hire someone based on religion or ethnicity—they're nevertheless issues whose resolution is urgent if Canada is to continue to invite immigrants with the promise that they'll find suitable employment when they arrive on these shores. This country must do a better job in delivering on the promises it makes when it opens its doors to the world.

For Canadian Muslims, the promise of economic success in Canada has yet to be truly fulfilled; when we look at their educational attainment and employment outcomes, we find a significant gap. Muslims in this country are better educated than the population at large: 45 percent hold a university degree as compared with 23 percent of all Canadians. And yet in terms of income, Muslim Canadians lag behind the national average.

It's true that Muslim Canadians face discrimination, unemployment, and underemployment—the state of being employed but not at a level that matches one's education and employment experience. But those issues must be considered in concert with their remarkably positive outlook on life in this country: their pride in Canada (which increases with time spent here) and their belief that their fellow Muslims wish to adapt to the Canadian way of life, that the country is on the right track, that only a small minority of Canadians are hostile to adherents of Islam, and that Muslims fare better in Canada than in other Western countries.

Taken together, these findings suggest that while Muslims are aware of and concerned about discrimination and economic challenges confronting their community, when they contextualize these worries as part of a larger experience of life in this country, life in their home countries, and life elsewhere in the West, they're hopeful about the future in Canada. This doesn't imply that prejudice and employment inequity don't require urgent attention. What it does suggest is that Muslim Canadians approach life in Canada with considerable optimism and goodwill—and see other Canadians as likely to try to meet them halfway. This is not the tinderbox of roiling dissatisfaction that leads to riots in the streets. It is, rather, a very strong starting point from which to pursue greater equality, better opportunities, and mutual understanding between Muslims and other Canadians.

I opened this chapter with a brief discussion about the hijab and the alarm it seems to induce in some Canadians, partly on grounds of gender equality. For those who imagine that Muslim Canadians are more intent on enforcing traditional gender roles than they are on having members of their community participate fully and equally in Canadian social, economic, and community life, consider this: when we asked Muslim Canadians to state their level of concern about six different issues relating to their life in this country, the changing role of women was at the bottom. Only one in ten Canadian Muslims were very worried about "Muslim women in Canada taking on modern roles in society," and fully half (48 percent) said they were "not at all worried" about this. Another quarter (24 percent) were "not too worried." Immigrants expect change when they move to a foreign country with a different culture. Adjustment may be difficult, but only a misguided person would move across the world and expect to find things as they were at home. Most newcomers to Canada understand that they and their families will have to adjust to new roles and social mores in their adoptive country; some may have difficulty making the change—and the younger generation often bear the brunt of the transition—but in general, human beings find ways to adapt, especially here in Canada.

THE SECURITY ELEPHANT

For some readers, the elephant sitting in the middle of this chapter is terrorism. If relations between Muslims and other Canadians are going so swimmingly, these people wonder, why were eighteen men and boys arrested in Mississauga, Ontario, in 2006 on charges of plotting terrorist acts against Canadian targets? Neither survey research nor census data can give us the answer to the truly dumbfounding questions we all have about brutality in general and terrorism in particular. How small numbers of people, usually young men, arrive—psychologically, emotionally, politically—at acts of numbing violence is beyond this pollster's margin of error. (Similarly, while I could discuss at miserable length differences in men's and women's values, attitudes, and opinions in this country, I could never tell you from my research how a Marc Lépine comes into existence—or where the next one might appear.)

What is *not* beyond my margin of error is to represent, as well as my data will allow, the views of the vast majority of Muslims in this country. When we look at these views, we can conclude only that the young men who were allegedly plotting violence—and those who allegedly encouraged them—are (if the allegations prove true) well outside the mainstream of Canadian Islam.

We asked Canadian Muslims if, hypothetically, terrorist attacks had been carried out against Canadian targets, whether those attacks would have been justified. Twelve percent said the attacks would have been at least somewhat justified. Five percent said they would have been completely justified. In another question, we asked—regardless of the extent to which the attacks were justified—whether people had any sympathy with the feelings or motives of the alleged plotters. Nine percent told us they had some sympathy with the young men who were allegedly plotting attacks.

These numbers may sound larger than we might like: in *The Edmonton Sun,* Licia Corbella wrote that these findings were appalling—that if 10 percent of Canadian Muslims thought terrorism was justified, this meant that (after a little napkin math around the margin of error) at least forty-nine thousand Muslims in this country were just waiting for a chance to strap on explosives.[1] But the link between opinion and action isn't so straightforward. For example, about 10 percent of all Canadians believe that non-whites shouldn't be allowed to immigrate to this country.[2] Another 10 percent believe that "it is acceptable to use physical force to get something you want. The important thing is to get what you want."[3] Ten percent believe that people who contracted HIV/AIDS through sex or drug use "got what they deserve."[4] Consider how profoundly marginal these positions are in Canadian society. Not only would they never be advanced by any politician, in most settings it would be social suicide for a private citizen to utter them aloud. Although they do exist and we may have even heard them expressed at some point, they're profoundly unacceptable in the Canadian mainstream.

Moreover, to say one has sympathy for someone doesn't necessarily mean one would encourage their behaviour. I have sympathy for young people who commit crimes. I condemn their crimes and generally believe they should be punished, but I can also remember doing rash, foolish things as a young man. I was smart enough (or more likely lucky enough) never to have been led by teenage testosterone to kill someone by drag racing or to seriously injure another kid in a fight. But I sympathize with some of the young people who stain their own lives forever by engaging in such behaviour, particularly when I read profiles that suggest they were heaped with disadvantages almost from birth and sometimes before that.

One can imagine some Canadian Muslims sympathizing with the frustrations of young people who feel their coreligionists are being unfairly treated, without actually advocating the violence that those young people were allegedly planning. To interpret this 10 percent as a group of fifty thousand would-be terrorists is dubious at best, and certainly alarmist journalism. None of this is to equivocate about terrorism itself.

While we find that approval of violence is a very marginal position in the Muslim community in this country, we also find that it's something Muslims themselves take very seriously. When we ask whether ordinary, law-abiding Muslims have any responsibility to report on potentially violent extremists in their communities, nearly nine in ten (87 percent) say they have a responsibility to do so—and seven in ten (72 percent) say they have a great deal of responsibility.

When I've described this latter question to some people, they've exclaimed that the very question might be considered offensive. How would I, raised a Christian, feel if someone called me at home and asked me if I felt responsible for the actions of religious extremists in the United States who shoot doctors who perform abortions? Or whether I felt responsible for the Oklahoma City bombing, perpetrated by one of "my people"—a white Christian male? I might find the very question either laughable or worthy of a rapid hang-up. But Canadian Muslims answered—and answered that they felt they *did* have a responsibility to be watchful of extremism.

This is not a book about Muslims and it's definitely not a book about terrorism. (Indeed, as I argue in my concluding chapter, to mingle the debate about security with discourse about multiculturalism and migration is a flawed way to approach both issues.) But I offer these findings as a corrective to those who imagine that the Canadian Muslim community is a minority group rife with extremism and sympathy for terror. The vast majority of Canadian Muslims, like most Canadian newcomers of other faiths or no faith, are here to build better lives for themselves and their children—not to dismantle Canadian society by violence. Even if—heaven forbid—a terrorist plot should occur in this country in the future, *this will still be true.*

FOR ALL THE JOURNALISTIC TALK about Islam in Canada—whether it be about a girl wearing a hijab on a soccer field, women voting in niqabs or burqas in Quebec, or the spectre of terrorism carried out in Canada under the banner of Islam—there tends to be very little discussion of what Canada's Muslim population actually looks like. Here are some things we learned from our research.

Muslims currently constitute only about 2.5 percent of the total population (according to Statistics Canada projections, there are 842,200 Muslims in Canada, of a total population of 33,099,000). Despite its small share of the overall religious pie in Canada, Islam is the fastest-growing religion in this country, and the median age of Canadian Muslims is about a decade lower than the median age of the population at large. In other words, Muslims are becoming an increasingly significant element of Canada's population.

Canadian Muslims, like Canadians overall, are diverse. As noted above, about 90 percent are foreign-born, and hail from all over the world. Their most frequently cited nations of origin are Pakistan and Iran, but these two countries combined account for only a fifth of the Muslim population. Canadian adherents of Islam come from more than thirty countries across Asia, Africa, and Europe: from Morocco to Iraq, from Bosnia to Ethiopia, from Turkey to Bangladesh.

Although, as I've noted elsewhere, Muslims are more highly

educated than the general population, their incomes are relatively low: 62 percent of Canadian Muslims have annual household incomes of less than $60,000. By comparison, this is true of just 44 percent of Canadians at large.

Two-thirds of Canadian Muslims (65 percent) are Sunni and 15 percent are Shia. Smaller proportions belong to the Ahmadi (2 percent), Ismaili (2 percent), Sufi (less than 1 percent), or other sects.

Among foreign-born Muslims, about half (51 percent) have come to Canada in the last ten years. Thirty percent have been in Canada for eleven to nineteen years, and 17 percent have been in this country for two decades or longer.

Most Canadian Muslims (60 percent) live in Ontario; for the most part, these people hail from Pakistan, Bangladesh, and Somalia. Twenty-one percent live in Quebec; these tend to be from French-speaking Morocco and Algeria. In the West, where 17 percent of Canada's Muslims live (yes, there really are little mosques on the Prairies; in fact, the first Canadian mosque was built in Edmonton in 1938), we find higher concentrations from Iran, Afghanistan, and Iraq.

Given the diversity of the Canadian Muslim community, generalizations about this community—any community— should be met with some caution. What is clear from our research, however, is that Muslims tend to share important traits with other newcomers to Canada: optimism, enthusiasm for their adopted country, a desire to improve their lives, and a wish to be treated fairly.

I will give the final word to Doug Saunders, writing in *The Globe and Mail*. After a thoughtful discussion of survey research and Muslim fertility rates in Europe, which are as low as in Canada, Saunders concludes that much of the talk about Muslims in the West—on topics ranging from religious fundamentalism to the Muslim baby boom that will supposedly overwhelm Europe—is ill-founded. "Once we get past the hysteria and look at the facts," he writes, "something becomes apparent about the Muslims: They're just like any group of immigrants, except for the stories we tell about them."[5]

Saunders's words hold every bit as true in Canada, his home and native land—indeed, maybe more so.

four

Quebec: The Distinct, Diverse Society

Vive le Québec! Vive le Québec libre!
—Charles de Gaulle, Montreal, 1967

L<small>IKE NEARLY EVERY OTHER REGION</small> in Canada, Quebec has changed dramatically in the last half-century. In the 1950s the English and the French were, in the oft-quoted words of novelist Hugh MacLennan, two solitudes sharing little more than the same air and tap water. The Anglos lived in their central- and west-end-Montreal enclaves and vacationed in the Eastern Townships while the francophones lived in Montreal's east end and dominated the rest of the province. The Anglos ruled the world of business and commerce. The Roman Catholic Church ruled most else, particularly educational institutions. The father of the family was master in his own house. And Maurice Duplessis, patriarch of the Union Nationale party, was the master of Quebec's political house in the legislative assembly.

Quebec was an insular society—albeit with strong ties to France, which francophones at the time perceived as their mother country. Some elites (or soon-to-be elites) were able to escape the great darkness, *la grande noirceur,* as the Duplessis era has been called. The peripatetic young Pierre Trudeau went to Harvard and the London School of Economics (LSE), and even future separatist premier Jacques Parizeau travelled to the Anglo mecca to earn a PhD in economics from LSE. But most Quebecers stayed home, where two stark camps abided: British and French (or "bloke" and "frog," as the epithets had it). To the extent that people with backgrounds other than British or French were recognized at all in the public imaginary, it was the Jews of European origin, many of whom had fled fascism and the Holocaust, and whose life in the Mile End neighbourhood was later caricatured in Technicolor by Mordecai Richler.

Toward the end of the 1950s it seemed to English Canada that a huge socio-cultural tsunami had crashed on the sleepy, pious province of Quebec. Duplessis died in 1959: the end of an era—perhaps even an epoch. The next year Liberal leader Jean Lesage propelled his party to a narrow but symbolically resounding victory and ushered in the Quiet Revolution. Quebecers were to become *maîtres chez nous:* masters in their own homeland. To observers inside Quebec the change was significant but not quite so surprising; they'd been watching urbanization, industrialization, the postwar economy, television, and other familiar drivers of change doing their work in Quebec as in the rest of North America. But from inside

Quebec or out, Canadians beheld the last days of the old duopoly: Anglos ruling commerce, the Church ruling the people, and the politicians brokering between the two and divvying up the patronage spoils among their supporters.

The current federal Liberal leader, Stéphane Dion, tells the story of his own deeply secular home, with a Quebec-born political science professor dad and a mom born in France (the latter yielding what would later become his controversial dual citizenship).[1] In the 1950s his family of non-religious intellectuals suffered ostracism for not attending Sunday morning mass—peers at school told little Stéphane that he would burn in hell. Then one day, Dion recalls, it seemed the entire province decided en masse to join him and his godless parents on the ski slopes rather than stay in church to line up for confession and communion.

Before the Quiet Revolution, national fellow-feeling in Quebec had been rooted in a common *pure laine* French ethnicity, the French language, and the Roman Catholic religion. Most francophones were employed in agriculture, resource industries, or at lower levels in the manufacturing and service economies, while the French elite found jobs in professions like law and medicine and, for the lucky few, politics. Education in the province was the domain of the Church. But with the Quiet Revolution came a new nationalism. It envisioned a future in which francophone Quebecers could excel in business and commerce, assuming power—not just political, but economic—in their own province. Secularism spread and, crucially, education became the responsibility of the state.

The Quiet Revolution affected all facets of life in Quebec, but it was in the political realm where its manifestations were the most strikingly evident. (Although I believe the abandonment of religion was more widespread and profound in its effects and implications.) The nationalism of the quiet political revolution bifurcated in the 1960s, as it had from time to time in Quebec since the Rebellion of 1837–38. One side remained Liberal; both in its provincial and federal arms, it was an assertion of the French fact within Quebec and within Canada. The other, sovereigntist strand emerged under the charismatic René Lévesque and other separatist leaders. This group broke away from the Liberals and transformed the inward-looking nationalism that had characterized French Quebec since the conquest in 1759 into an increasingly self-confident movement that aspired to political power and the eventual independence of Quebec.

One product of this newly confident Quebec was federal acknowledgment of Canada's bilingualism. The Royal Commission on Bilingualism and Biculturalism, launched by Prime Minister Lester Pearson's government in 1963, resulted in the 1969 Official Languages Act guaranteeing that Canadians could receive government services in either French or English, where population size warranted. With the communion host now absent from the tongues of Quebec Catholics, the tongue itself became a preoccupation; language was to dominate the political debate for a generation.

A byproduct of the commission—a byproduct whose relevance to the Canada of the future almost no one could have fully foreseen in the year the commission issued its report—was an acknowledgment that while Canada had two official languages, it had more than two cultures. This recognition of the multicultural fact of Canada—the fact that fully a quarter of the non-Aboriginal population was of neither British nor French heritage—was certainly not a project spearheaded by Quebecers. Far from seeing themselves as just one of the gang, francophone Quebecers conceived of themselves as one of two founding nations—*deux peuples fondateurs*. The dualistic conception of Canada was powerful in Quebec, although whether to remain yoked to or break away from the other founding nation was, of course, another matter.

The idea of multiculturalism was invented in Ottawa not with Quebec in mind but rather to mollify groups of neither British nor French origin—particularly Ukrainians in the Prairies—who balked at the idea of Canada's being officially proclaimed a place of two languages and two cultures. The non-British, non-French part of the equation was recognized in Book Four of the report of the Royal Commission on

Bilingualism and Biculturalism, entitled with rather inglorious vagueness "The Cultural Contributions of Other Groups."

Multiculturalism was of marginal interest to the small population of so-called allophones (those whose first language was neither English nor French) who lived mainly in Montreal, and was of no interest to the vast majority of Quebecers who were either francophones or anglophones. Anglophones were largely the descendants of English and Scottish immigrants and certainly didn't think of themselves as an ethnic minority. They enjoyed substantial wealth and power in Quebec—they were a minority, but an elite one—and weren't likely to imagine that their kilted pipers might line up alongside dancing Ukrainians for a slice of multicultural largesse. The other famous Quebec minority, Montreal's European Jews, would have been similarly unlikely to apply for a multicultural grant to fund their uniqueness. They suffered plenty of discrimination and were a minority twice over—the saying went that if anglophones were a pocket in Quebec, Jews were a stitch in the pocket—but they weren't vocal proponents of multiculturalism as were westerners of Eastern European descent. In other words, arousing little interest from either the French majority or the non-French minorities, multiculturalism was largely irrelevant in Quebec.

The preoccupation of Quebec politicians wasn't the accommodation or celebration of ethnocultural differences, but rather the preservation of the embattled French language in North America. Instead of helping younger generations remain connected to their Old World heritage, the Quebec government was intent on establishing laws and policies to ensure that the children of allophones and immigrants received French-language education. The culmination of this aspiration was the monumental Bill 101 passed by the separatist Parti Québécois in 1977—shortly after its first election victory in November 1976.

The insistence on French as the official language in Quebec, and efforts to make public education fall in line with this new fact, have meant two things for immigration and multiculturalism in Quebec and in Canada at large: that a disproportionately small number of immigrants settle in Quebec, and that a disproportionate share of Quebec's immigrants come from French-speaking countries, especially Haiti but also North African countries such as Algeria and Morocco. As we saw in the introduction, the source countries of immigration to Canada have shifted dramatically over the past half-century: from Christian Europe prior to 1960 to African and especially Asian countries in recent decades. And if adapting to this pattern of immigration has been a challenge for Canadians living outside Quebec, the challenge has been much greater for those inside Canada's distinct society.

It's quite remarkable: Quebec is renowned for being the

most flexible, progressive region of North America with regard to social values, and yet it registers more anxiety than the rest of Canada over its religious and ethnocultural minorities. When people discuss the differences in values between Canada and the United States, they often say, "Oh—the two countries are the same, it's only Quebec's distinct values that pull Canada away from our American cousins." While there is much evidence to suggest there's more to the story of Canada and the United States, these critics are right about Quebec: *la belle province* stands out as extremely liberal, relative to both the United States and to English Canada. Quebecers have flexible and open attitudes on all kinds of values, from family and religion to sexuality and personal identity.

And yet. In Environics polling, seven in ten Quebecers (70 percent) agree that "there are too many immigrants coming into this country who are not adopting Canadian values." Forty-three percent agree strongly with this statement. The proportion of Canadians outside Quebec who agree with the statement is five points lower, with 38 percent agreeing strongly.[2] When we surveyed Canadians on their attitudes toward Muslims in this country, Quebecers were the most likely (67 percent) to believe that Canadian Muslims wanted to remain distinct from the larger society. Outside Quebec, the proportion of Canadians who believed that Muslims wish to remain apart was closer to half: 54 percent. In addition, when

we ask Canadians whether a French-style ban (in public institutions) on the head scarves worn by some Muslim women is
a good idea, over half of Quebecers (54 percent) support the
idea as compared with just three in ten (31 percent) of those
outside Quebec. And while this might seem to indicate a
particular suspicion of Muslims—perhaps a post-9/11 fear of
terror—Quebecers are in fact the least likely of all Canadians
to express high levels of concern about terrorism in Canada.

Taken together, I read these findings thus: Quebecers'
enthusiasm for a head scarf ban appears to stem from their
feeling culturally threatened by minority groups in their
province, and as a result they wish to apply pressure against the
expression of minority religious and cultural identities. But it
appears *not* to stem from any specifically anti-Muslim sentiment. After all, the case of the Sikh boy wearing a kirpan to
school and the Jewish group that wanted the neighbouring
YMCA to tint its windows caused widespread controversy in
Quebec. (They caused talk elsewhere, too, but the cases arose
in Quebec and it was there that they were debated most
fiercely.)

Clearly, Quebecers' concern about how newcomers and
minority groups are affecting Quebec society isn't solely a
matter of language, that is, the desire for immigrants to adopt
French as their second language if it's not already their first.
Certainly, many Quebecers would prefer that allophone immi-

grants learn French rather than English. But as much as language, values seem to concern Quebecers. I believe Quebecers worry that immigrants won't adopt the dominant cultural values of Quebec, values that have changed more quickly and more dramatically in this little corner of the world than perhaps anywhere else west of the Urals.

In the middle part of the twentieth century, Quebecers underwent a massive socio-cultural upheaval. They rejected a Roman Catholicism that had suffused every bit of their life as a people. They also asserted a shared political identity as Québécois, challenging not only the economic and political dominance of Anglos in the province but also proclaiming more emphatically a socio-cultural identity that was decidedly un-WASP. Between these two movements, Quebecers grew into both a feeling and an expression of their identity that was not only new and unique but hard-won. And so what Quebecers are concerned about today is that large numbers of immigrants to their province are clinging to precisely those kinds of traditional values that Quebecers rejected so vehemently and so universally a generation ago. Our data show that immigrant groups embrace religiosity and patriarchy much more strongly than those born in Canada do. For Quebecers, these traditional values were jettisoned with no small effort and at no small cost. To perceive—whether it's the case or not—a resurgence of traditional values in the province is to perceive a crack in the cool, *branché,* future-oriented identity Quebecers have claimed for themselves in the last several decades.

Yes, it's true that the Quiet Revolution also happened outside Quebec, but it happened more slowly and even more quietly. Ontario and other provinces had their share of Catholic kids who questioned the priest. Nor indeed was the rebellion limited to the Catholic Church; hundreds of thousands of young United Church, Anglican, Presbyterian, and other Protestant children rejected the faiths and rituals of their parents. In most cases people just drifted away, the pews depleting almost imperceptibly over time until now, a half-century later, conventional religious belief and practice have become the convention for only a minority of Canadians, fewer than one in four.

Quebecers not only rejected traditional religious ritual and conviction but also many conventions associated with the Church, like marriage and a wife's taking her husband's surname. Quebec came to have the highest proportion of common-law unions in Canada; in the rest of the country formal marriage remains the norm. Quebec is still the revolutionary leader in the rejection of religion and its symbolic trappings.

My friend and research colleague Alain Giguère (president of the Quebec polling firm CROP) and I discovered in adulthood that we must have rejected our inherited faith on almost exactly the same day—I as a boy from Walkerton, Ontario, and he in Joliette, Quebec. We each screwed up our courage and told our dads that we didn't wish to go to mass and communion any more. In my case, my dad (raised in the United Church) prevailed upon me to continue attending mass until I left home, if only to protect the feelings of my Roman Catholic mother who would have believed my loss of faith put her immortal soul in jeopardy—not to mention her standing in our faith community. Alain, like so many of his peers, responded more categorically to a far more authoritarian and domineering Catholic clergy, which had once infamously (in the election of 1896) told congregations across the province how they should vote. Alain and a whole generation of young Quebecers felt the collective emotional liberation that flows from an anti-clerical revolution. Quebec's revolution involved no loss of life, but it was pretty exciting by Canadian standards.

The emotion that propelled Quebecers into their sometimes unquiet revolution against the Church later transformed itself into the nationalism of the 1960s. From the rejection of the Church, Quebecers moved to the embrace of the state and of their shared ethnolinguistic identity. The state replaced the Church as a source of comfort and even meaning; Quebecers went from the hope of everlasting life to the expectation of cradle-to-grave social security—and the assertion of the French fact. Quebec became a secular, egalitarian society where liberal social values, sexual liberation, soft hedonism, and tolerance for an increasing variety of lifestyles and identities prevailed. The sleepy little province had evolved from tradition to modernity to postmodernity at socio-cultural warp speed in just half a century.

I would argue, then, that two factors account for Quebec's higher levels of concern about the social and cultural influence of newcomers and minority groups. First, there is Quebecers' long-standing anxiety about the preservation of their own minority culture and the survival of the French language in North America. Second, I believe that the speed and insistence with which Quebecers rejected traditional religious values can account to a great extent for the pitch of their worry about an influx of traditional religious values and practices from elsewhere in the world. It is my belief that the majority of Quebecers are incorrect in their perception that newcomers don't wish to participate fully in Canadian and Québécois social, economic, and political life. But I believe it is this perception that is nevertheless driving some of the reaction we've seen against assertions of minority identity and religious practice in Quebec.

The paradoxical desire to protect and preserve a culture of openness and flexibility is by no means unique to Quebec. Perhaps the most potent distillate of this phenomenon was the political career of Pim Fortuyn in the Netherlands. Fortuyn, often described as a far-right politician in the manner of Jean-Marie Le Pen of France or Jörg Haider of Austria, was violently opposed to immigration. Not only did he think his country should cease to accommodate even asylum seekers, he said that if he could halt all Muslim immigration to the Netherlands he would. But Fortuyn wasn't a stereotypical right-winger. He was openly gay, and the thing he thought he might protect by excluding immigrants from his country was the Netherlands' famously liberal social climate and policies: gay rights, women's rights, and legal marijuana and prostitution. In 2002 Fortuyn was assassinated by, of all people, an animal rights activist. With the death of its charismatic leader, his party, the Pim Fortuyn List, had dwindled to nothing by 2006.

There is no politician like Pim Fortuyn in Quebec—or anywhere else in Canada. But the belief that our open, egalitarian social climate must be protected against outsiders with less open, egalitarian values is certainly present in this country. This mindset can be especially potent when the idea of what "us" and "our" mean is stronger and more coherent. In Quebec, fully 70 percent of the population claim French ancestry, have French as their mother tongue, *and* have family heritage in Quebec stretching back three generations or more. This is a province that, although diverse, has a dominant ethnic and linguistic majority—a "nous."

In English Canada, by contrast, the proportion of the population that might be classified as *pure laine* WASP is 20 percent.[3] Yes, the rest of Canada is still mostly white, but the diversity within that white majority—a diversity of ethnocultural heritage, language, and religion—is tremendous. There is simply no sense of a core *people* in English Canada any more. There is a political entity called Canada, and a society in which many of us, of all backgrounds, are deeply invested. But the sense of an "us" that might be threatened by "them" is a very hard sell in this country, where everyone— even the once mighty WASP—is a small minority.

Although Quebec is increasingly diverse, that province can still perceive in itself a majority "us." In this sense, Quebec may resemble a European country with a somewhat monocultural past—though clearly not a monocultural future— more than it does the rest of Canada. Like much of Western Europe—sometimes referred to as "post-Christian"—Quebec has evolved from religiosity and patriarchy to a secular hedonism that tolerates, accommodates, and even celebrates traditional vices in a spirit of live and let live. And like many Western Europeans, Quebecers worry that anyone who isn't cool with all this may be a threat to their evolving postmodern utopia. Unlike many European countries, Quebec is used to significant amounts of immigration—so knee-jerk xenophobia in the province is minimal. But also unlike many Europeans,

Quebecers have arrived at their current sublime refinement not only by overthrowing their own fathers and priests but also by asserting their identity in the face of a historical Anglo elite.

So Quebecers may well be justified in feeling they have something to protect, but protecting it from what and from whom will be urgent and thorny questions for the province in the years to come. How this will play out politically remains to be seen, although the spring 2007 election, in which politicians jockeyed to be seen as standing firm against the supposed threats and demands of minority groups, may have been a taste of things to come.

Yet when Quebecers say they embrace the concept of reasonable accommodation it's not code for assimilation, nor is it an invitation to immigrants to form monocultural enclaves or impoverished ghettos. It's a version of the multiculturalism we see in Toronto, Vancouver, and elsewhere. It asks different groups to live where they wish, but to speak the French language and to adapt in symbolic ways to the hedonism and tolerance that have become the new French fact in Quebec.

Yes there have been tragic shootings in Quebec as elsewhere and yes they may have given expression, as *Globe and Mail* journalist Jan Wong has infamously suggested, to some element of exclusion. But marginal youth, specifically marginal male youth, have resorted to homicide and suicide for a very long time and in myriad contexts and with a bewildering array of motives. To indict a culture because of a few scattered incidents is problematic; to question a culture when such incidents become a pattern is legitimate. But we have not yet come close to that point anywhere in Canadian society, including Quebec, at least not when it comes to questioning the ideals of multiculturalism.

In this regard, distinct Quebec is on the same trajectory as the rest of Canada. The difference is that given the rapidity of social change and the perceived fragility of Quebec culture, there is seen to be more at stake—and therefore a more potent emotion tends to be expressed in the province's discourse. Quebec, like Canada, has always accepted large numbers of immigrants. Although there is no question that those newcomers have had a unique experience in Canada's distinct society (likely to their gastronomic benefit), they have also been living in Canada: with its Charter, its laws, its health care, its passport, and its people.

Whether Quebec stays, leaves, or, in some constitutional contortion, both stays *and* leaves, the trajectory of reasonable accommodation will continue in that province/nation/country because immigration will always be a factor in Quebec life. The demography of declining fertility demands it. And just as the rest of Canada will continue to be itself—not the UK, not France, not Australia—Quebec will not be the Netherlands. It will be Quebec.

Conclusion
Working on Utopia

We need a sense of justice, but we also need common sense;
we need imagination, a deep ability to imagine the other,
sometimes to put ourselves in the skin of the other.
[I prescribe] imagining the other and a sense of humor. Not as
a substitute for real compromise but as a preparation.

—Amos Oz, *How to Cure a Fanatic*

It is my experience that books on contemporary politics and social trends rarely pass the test of time. The predictions of the pundits, pollsters, and trend watchers often prove not only wrong but downright irrelevant. The certainties and anxieties of one period are quickly displaced by events that almost no one could have predicted. The world of ideas is not so different from the futuristic fashion landscape of the original *Star Trek:* predictions usually tell us much more about the time in which they were created than they do about the future we actually experience.

Even the work of great historians, deciphering the events of the past with the power of retrospection, is rarely the last word on anything. We're bound to see the past through a changing lens as time advances; debates thought to be long settled can be reopened by contrarians, ideologues, new science, or other innovations or discoveries. We all hope that

the lens through which we view the past becomes continu-
ally clearer, broader, more revealing. But the best we can do,
really, is try to remind ourselves that the lens—whatever its
properties—exists.

This book isn't the work of a historian or a futurist; it is the
work of a pollster who, though decidedly not an academic, at
times aspires to be considered a social scientist. Books by pollsters are especially vulnerable to being prisoners of their
context because the pollster's job is to reflect, as accurately as
possible, public concerns and perceptions at a particular point
in time. Even last night's poll is history.

I am well aware of the dangers of polling punditry. It took
me two and a half decades after cofounding my company in
1970, and a lot of coaxing, to try to make sense of and write
about all the polls and surveys we (and others) had conducted
over the years. I published *Sex in the Snow* in 1997 because I
thought our data offered an interesting window onto the
evolution of Canadian social values—that they offered
evidence of an underlying narrative in the story of modern
Canada. I was certainly not the only one to perceive the core
elements of this narrative—growing secularism and declining
deference among Canadians—but I was fortunate enough to
have amassed with my colleagues a unique stash of evidence of
Canadians' evolving values. Part of what made our research
unusual was that my associates and I had developed a

psychographic segmentation of the Canadian public in the contemporary context of changing values.

Sex in the Snow argued that demography was no longer destiny. Knowing someone's gender, age, or ethnicity might tell you something about a person, but not as much as it once did. The reason is that our life choices are increasingly dictated by our values and ever less influenced by biological imperatives and tribal allegiances. This may seem obvious today, but just half a century ago a female who pursued a career outside nursing or teaching was an oddity, and a woman who didn't have children was viewed as almost pathologically contrary (or unable to find a man). My own mother aspired to become a doctor but was informed rather emphatically by her own father that women who wanted to be involved in medicine became nurses. My brainy, energetic mum became a nurse: demographic predestination in action, enforced by traditional values.

Embedded in the idea that values were increasingly shaping people's lives was the one that people were becoming more autonomous: we weren't just collections of ascribed demographic characteristics, we were individuals with desires, opinions, beliefs, and emotions—all of which we wanted to express in the way we lived our lives. Which is not to say we wanted to live lives of untrammelled individualism. (After all, we needed an audience so that we could show off all our choices.)

What we wanted was autonomy and interdependence: to be ourselves within the context of norms, rules, laws, and institutions that still served to give meaning and structure to our lives. In other words, we wanted to be ourselves among others who would respect our choices.

I believe that Canadian multiculturalism—and by multiculturalism I mean the demographic reality as well as the policy framework—is an outgrowth of the increasing sense of autonomy and interdependence I've explored in my writing since the first draft of *Sex in the Snow*. Only in a place where people have by and large adopted a live-and-let-live approach to social existence can multiculturalism really flourish. Naturally, living and letting live doesn't solve everything; people can "let [others] live" in poverty while they themselves "mind their own business" in neighbourhoods, workplaces, and institutions of privilege. But the basic principle of autonomy, that individuals and communities can live as they choose provided they can respect one another and follow the rules, is the soil in which any society that is both diverse and harmonious must plant itself.

Some readers have now begun to roll their eyes. It's all fine and well, they're thinking, to talk about respect and rules—but what are the specifics? Where do we draw the lines? The concern is sometimes expressed that there are no boundaries to Canadian multiculturalism—that minority communities can engage in any behaviour, even very objectionable behaviour, and defend it on the grounds of culture or heritage or religion. Indeed, the following description of multiculturalism, by British writer Melanie Phillips, was published in the *National Post* in the wake of the Mississauga arrests:

> At the heart of multiculturalism lies a radical egalitarianism by which everyone's culture and lifestyle has equal validity and moral stature. The consequence is that people are increasingly unable to make moral distinctions based on behaviour. Instead, minorities of all kinds— ethnic, religious, sexual—are not held responsible for their misdeeds because they are perceived as a victim class.

Homing in on the group she's really talking about, Phillips concludes that

> Canada, like all Western nations, should send a clear message that while Islam is respected like any minority faith, Muslims must play by the rules of the minority game. That means that our countries will not allow religion to be used to incite hatred and violence, and where this is taking place—in mosques or madrassahs, in prisons, youth clubs or on campus—it will be

stopped. But that can only happen if the shibboleth of multiculturalism is set aside.[1]

Only when Canada has set aside multiculturalism, Phillips claims, can this country stand firm in upholding principles of democracy against an onslaught of barbarism from elsewhere. This kind of talk implies that multiculturalism somehow exempts people from the rule of law. In fact it does no such thing. Multiculturalism implies some flexibility in allowing minority groups access to the benefits enjoyed by their fellow citizens—like government jobs (which is why you can wear a turban and still be a Mountie). But multiculturalism certainly isn't a free pass to murder and mayhem or even to hate speech. The rules are the rules—yes, for everyone.

And what are the rules that everyone agrees to follow? The answers to this question are simpler than people sometimes imagine. The rules we all agree most seriously to follow— whatever our country of origin, religion, race, gender, sexual orientation, political beliefs, or any other marker—are Canada's laws. Our *existing* laws. For example, contrary to what the Herouxville councillors appeared to imagine, stoning women is already illegal throughout Canada. No one so far has received an exemption on religious or "multicultural" grounds. (Though I suppose a little municipal redundancy in this regard can't do any harm.) To hear people like Melanie

Phillips tell it, you'd think Canada faces an influx of especially violent newcomers whose behaviour our existing legal framework is ill-equipped to address. This is obviously false. We have laws, and immigrants come here agreeing to follow them. If individuals of any religious or ethnic background don't follow the laws, they're charged and, if found guilty, prosecuted. It really is that simple.

Herouxville may seem a frivolous example, but the Herouxville declaration obviously expressed a certain anxiety about whether any firm rules exist in Canada. The implicit question was, Will Canadians, in their efforts to be "tolerant" and their desire not to appear racist, tolerate any behaviour at all? The answer is, and has always been, no.

The often-cited conflict between the individual rights we all enjoy as Canadians and the group rights ethnocultural communities enjoy under multiculturalism is hardly the nation-rending question it's sometimes positioned as. As Will Kymlicka has argued so lucidly, no real tension prevails between multiculturalism and individual rights:

> The model of multiculturalism in Canada supports the ability of immigrants to choose for themselves whether to maintain their ethnic identity. There is no suggestion that ethnic groups should have the power to impose a conception of cultural tradition or cultural purity on their

members, or to interfere with the freedom of individual members to accept or reject their ethnic identity. The line that has been drawn in Canada—rejecting internal restrictions while accepting some external protections—is neither arbitrary nor ad hoc. It is just what one would expect in a liberal democracy.[2]

Can a minority religious group make a claim, on the grounds of multiculturalism, that its members should not (for example) be penalized for missing school or work on a religious holiday that is not a Canadian statutory holiday? Yes. This allows those *individuals* (who may have formed a group to voice and advocate for their religious needs) to practise their religion freely without being penalized in the Canadian educational or economic system. Can a patriarchal religious community leader make a claim, on the grounds of multiculturalism, to deny a girl from his community access to education? No way. The girl's rights as a Canadian unambiguously trump the religious leader's claims.

It is thanks to the clear primacy of the Charter that some Muslim women, concerned about some applications of Sharia law, nevertheless chose to advocate for Sharia's official recognition as a mechanism for settling family disputes in Ontario. They believed that Sharia-based family arbitration, carried out openly and publicly, would both accommodate the religious wishes of Muslims (those who chose to engage in the voluntary religious arbitration) and protect their Charter rights. Some even hoped that the application of Sharia law under provincial government scrutiny would help to start reconciling Sharia itself with life in modern societies—that Sharia law as applied in Canada might even become a model for its practice in other parts of the world.

For a bunch of supposedly spineless liberal wimps, we're pretty tough when it comes to our Charter of Rights and Freedoms. Canadians take very seriously its guarantee of religious freedom, of gender equality, and above all of security of the person. (Which is one reason why you can't apply for a permit to stone someone in the town square—in Herouxville or anywhere else in our dominion.)

The Canadian commitment to equality and rejection of discrimination is anything but spineless. There is nothing about this country that I'm more sure of. And indeed, when we survey newcomers to this country it's precisely these qualities—democracy, freedom, equality, and rights—that they appreciate most about Canada. The idea that these principles of equality are under assault by people who hail from different traditions—and that those of us who value equality are too timid or relativistic to defend it—is nonsense. Canadians know very well how to sustain their laws and their principles, and the vast majority of those who come to this country from elsewhere have no wish to dismantle them anyway.

I'm not suggesting that immigrants from different traditions—with different political systems, different religions, different cultural mores—arrive in Canada and automatically shed all their expectations about religious practice, gender norms, politics, and so on. Polling shows that newcomers today are by and large more traditional in their values than are people born here. Immigrants tend to be more deferential to patriarchal authority, more religious, and less flexible on issues of family and sexuality. Religion is protected under our Charter, and secular bigotry is also permissible within limits. No one can insist that newcomers, or anyone else, abandon whatever patriarchy or homophobia some may espouse. Canadians, whether they've been here for generations or got their citizenship last week, are entitled to certain rights and freedoms—and thus are free to entertain certain prejudices within certain parameters. (For example, Canadians can't deny people jobs or housing or try to incite violence against them on grounds of race, religion, gender, or sexual orientation.)

Immigrants tend to know this before they come to Canada. Sure, they come here for a better life, starting with a good job. But they also know that this is a modern, secular culture. If they have kids and have done any research at all, they know their children will likely go to publicly funded schools with

other Canadian kids of various religious and ethnic backgrounds, and that the language of instruction will be English
or French. Like all parents, they hope their children will do
well in school, get good jobs, and live happy lives. Maybe they
hope, as my grandparents did, that whatever influences their
kids encounter in the broader society, they'll wind up marrying
within their own ethnic or religious group. When my Catholic
mother and Protestant father married in Walkerton, Ontario,
in 1945, it raised plenty of eyebrows, including their parents'.
One generation on, I won't be surprised or dismayed if either
of my kids brings home a person of any background, or either
gender. Contexts change. Values change. People change.

Sometimes the changes—especially intergenerational
ones—can be tremendously painful within individual families.
When fathers are not only struggling to support their families
in a challenging new social and economic context but also
feeling the authority they may have enjoyed in their country of
origin challenged, serious conflict—even tragedy—can result.
Not every story of Old World meeting New reaches a happy
Bend It like Beckham conclusion. But newcomer families,
like other families, generally negotiate, ignore, cajole, and
compromise their way to a solution everyone can live with.

As the great sociologist Irving Goffman observed, individuals often bear the brunt of colliding social systems. Some
teenagers act as unwitting ambassadors for intergenerational

social change every time they walk through the front door of their parents' homes. Many newcomers experience tremendous personal upheaval as they negotiate a new culture. Much of the fallout of cultural collisions occurs fairly quietly, in the private lives of individuals and families. (This is one reason why literature about migration is often so rich: breathtaking stories can arise when cultures meet one another in the landscape of a single person's emotional, intellectual, and spiritual life.)

The fact that migration is difficult shouldn't be news to anyone. People who choose to immigrate to a far-off country with unfamiliar languages, climates, and customs are generally prepared to meet these challenges because they anticipate certain rewards. Those rewards are primarily economic opportunities and, in some cases, improved social and political circumstances. What newcomers are not—and should not be—prepared to deal with is denial of the very economic opportunities that brought them there in the first place.

With its points system and its proactive recruitment of immigrants (particularly economic-class immigrants) from around the world, Canada promises that people who move to this country and contribute to its economy will be rewarded with remunerative, fulfilling jobs commensurate with their qualifications. They will have to learn an official language, they will have to follow the rules, and they will have to endure some upheaval, but they'll live in a generally safe, peaceful country where they'll make a good living and their kids will enjoy a bright future. If this promise proves true, or mostly true, people's natural resiliency will help them through the rough patches that inevitably accompany migration. If this promise is false, the rough patches will be devastating—because overcoming them will seem futile.

As I cited earlier, the Statistics Canada report released in spring 2007 revealed that after two years in Canada, only a third (35 percent) of economic-class immigrants reported that their material well-being had improved over their situation in their country of origin. Yet there are other, more hopeful signs: after four years most of these people felt that their material circumstances were continuing to improve, and even at the two-year mark a large majority said that even if they were struggling financially their overall quality of life was better in Canada. Still, making good on the promise of economic opportunity is clearly a key challenge for Canada if it wants to help immigrants adjust successfully to life in their new country.

The Western world has been much preoccupied with terrorist attacks on civilian targets as it has watched events unfold in New York, Washington, Madrid, and London. Because some of the men involved in these attacks spent considerable time in the West (most notably the London bombers, who were raised in the UK), discussions of terrorism have become entangled with those of migration and multiculturalism. And when the riots in Paris and the ethnic clashes in Sydney are cited in the same breath as the London bombings, they're all framed as instances of minority groups (especially disaffected young men) lashing out against adoptive societies that have either failed to treat them fairly, offended their rigid religious values, or both.

But this muddying of the distinction between terrorism born of ideology and riots born of social and economic frustration is deeply problematic. International terrorism carried out under the banner of Islam, whatever its deepest causes, is different from the Paris riots in a couple of ways. First, terrorism can be carried out by anyone; as we are constantly told, it's an international project. If Osama bin Laden wants New Yorkers or Londoners or Torontonians to die because of their governments' foreign policies, he has a whole world in which to find or cultivate like-minded people who will perpetrate attacks. He doesn't need young men in Queens or Leeds or Mississauga; he can recruit them from pretty well anywhere. Pluralism in Western countries need not be failing in order for terrorism to be unleashed against Western targets. If an attack occurs in Toronto next week it will be a terrible tragedy and an appalling crime, but it won't necessarily say anything at all about Canadian multiculturalism.

Second, the objectives of organizations like al Qaeda seem to have nothing to do with the well-being of Muslims or other minority groups living in Western societies. Sure, the causes that spur people to become involved in terrorist activity are difficult to pinpoint with certainty; perhaps the young men involved in the London bombings, for example, were frustrated by social or economic exclusion they experienced in England and somehow sublimated that frustration into religious conviction or violent rage or something else. But it remains true that terrorist attacks against Western targets have not been carried out haphazardly; they've been perpetrated against countries whose foreign policy certain militant leaders find objectionable. The list of marked countries is public. The reasons for the marking are public. Osama bin Laden in his public remarks hasn't expressed much worry about whether newcomers to Canada have their foreign credentials recognized or whether PhDs are driving taxis or whether there are ethnic enclaves in the suburbs of Vancouver. The terrorist project—however incomprehensible in its violence and extremism—does operate by a political logic. And that logic has nothing to do with the treatment of Muslims or any other minority groups in Western societies.

In this book I argue that diversity is basically working in Canada. It's not perfect, but it's on the right track. If—horribly—a terrorist attack does occur on Canadian soil, there is no need to throw out this book; nothing in it will necessarily have been proven false. But if one day you wake up and read on the front page of the newspaper that tens of thousands of cars have been burned by angry, excluded youth in the suburbs of a Canadian city where unemployment among ethnic minorities approaches 40 percent, by all means throw the book out. I'll have already used mine as kindling.

Why is it important to make this distinction? Because while terrorist attacks don't really tell us much about how newcomers or minority groups are faring in a given society, events like the Paris riots most certainly do. And to the extent that we conflate the two, we lump in legitimate issues of fairness and social inclusion (in areas like employment opportunities and political representation) with extremist ideologies that have no interest in such things. If every North African male youth in Paris had the same job opportunities as white French youth, felt he was treated fairly by the police, and felt fully a part of French society, the Paris riots would never have happened. But if the same were true of every Muslim living in the United States, 9/11 would very likely still have happened. Discussions about terrorism are important, but they're *not* at bottom discussions about migration, diversity, and multiculturalism.

One could argue that people sometimes collapse issues of multiculturalism and security out of simple xenophobia; that deep down, many people in Western societies believe that young men from elsewhere (and perhaps steeped in the religions and ideologies of elsewhere) are essentially dangerous and that in order to be neutralized they must be "assimilated." If those boys got out on the hockey rink and had some good clean fun, "they" would be more like "us" and everyone would be better off. This idea—however subtly stated—does underlie some of the discourse, particularly journalistic discourse, around security and diversity in Canada. It's not a very instructive way of thinking about either terrorism or pluralism.

But there is another, more legitimate reason why multiculturalism and security are sometimes discussed in the same breath in this country. It has to do with the ideas of social inclusion, belonging, and meaning in life. These ideas *are* somewhat related to the practice of multiculturalism in Canada—but are by no means limited to newcomer or minority ethnic communities. It's not very hard to find evidence that when people feel cut off from society, they can become dangerous. This is as true of the Oklahoma City bomber, Timothy McVeigh (remember what "homegrown terrorism" meant before 9/11?), or the Unabomber, Ted Kaczynski, or Montreal's Dawson College shooter Kimveer Gill as it is of any of the young men who blew themselves up in the London subway system. Young men can be dangerous creatures. One of society's central functions has always been to help them become men who exercise a minimum of violence (at least in their role as civilians) and a maximum of "productive" effort (economic activity, religious study, parenting, democratic engagement, or whatever).

How people can feel both free to be themselves and yet connected to others, autonomous yet guided by some sense of principle and common cause, is one of the great questions of postmodern secular societies. And it's a question that applies to all of us, not just religious or ethnic minorities. (Indeed, in many cases, belonging to a minority community may confer on many young people a sense of shared identity and pride that skeptical white kids of European origin—kids like mine—don't have.) Everyone is looking for meaning and a sense of identity. And this sense of identity can be rooted in anything from religion, ethnicity, and language to sexual orientation, country of origin, and disability. Online identities matter more and more: from avatars in elaborate computer games to blogging to chat-room personae, young people try on such a diversity of hats in their online lives that those of us who went through adolescence with one stark choice—jock or nerd?—can only marvel.

It doesn't take a prophet to predict that the cultural creativity arising from the collision of people of such diverse backgrounds living in a context where they can make such diverse choices will be astonishing. Because, of course, in addition to all the ascribed traits we talk about—religion, ethnicity, country of origin, and so on—there are the values-based tribal milieus I've described in my previous books. In this Canada, a person with a distinct demographic profile can no longer be assumed to be a simple mixture of such personal demographics as gender, age, and cultural and racial background. If you think people like Irshad Manji (a feminist, a lesbian, a Muslim) or Sheema Khan (who wears a hijab, has a PhD in chemical engineering, and founded the Harvard women's hockey team) are one-off eccentrics, think again. They are harbingers of an expanding range of possibilities for Canadians seeking to construct and express authentic identities.

Yes, some people will retrench, finding meaning by embracing traditional unitary identities rather than experimenting with the various personae—social, professional, cultural, even digital—that the world presents to them. This will be true of some first- or second-generation Canadians who decide, like Gogol Ganguli, the hero of Jhumpa Lahiri's novel *The Namesake,* that they want to embrace the customs and religion of their parents or grandparents—as identity, as political statement, as tribute, as performance, as whatever. It will also be true of some young people whose families have been in Canada for generations. I've spotted men in their twenties sporting baseball caps reading "Vimy Ridge: Birth of a Nation." These young men are also claiming a traditional identity: they want to fantasize about a tough old Canada for which real men like their grandfathers fought and died, in a time when men were men and women admired them. Fine. That's one way to be.

My pollster colleague Allan Gregg believes that if we're to be a nation, we can't all just drift about in our own tribes (metaphorical or literal), cliques, niches, and enclaves. In order to exist successfully as a collective—to have a shared sense of citizenship—we need defining ideals, national projects, grand designs. We need things we can all sign up for and hang our hats, turbans, and hijabs on. This might be a good idea, but what would it entail? Wars are national projects, but they tend not to be much fun. We built ourselves a big railway and that was a national project, but Chinese labourers didn't find it a very rewarding mechanism of social inclusion. We could all sign a document that expresses "Canadian values," but would that document be written by General Rick Hillier or comedian Rick Mercer?

The fact is, we already have a national project. And that project is the subject of this book. It is the effort to live in a country of peace and prosperity, with laws that are just, people who are humane, and where citizens of all backgrounds encounter equal opportunities when they set out to realize their potential, contribute to their communities, participate in the Canadian economy, and engage the Canadian political system. We don't all need to beat our chests to the same rhythm in order to be a great country. Quite the opposite, in fact: I believe Canada's success in welcoming newcomers can be largely attributed to the *absence* of national chauvinism in this country. Instead of expecting newcomers to conform to some already defined ideal of what it is to be Canadian, Canada seems to say, "Come here and we'll build Canada together." For as long as we've been a country, we've debated what we are. We've often doubted that there's a "we" at all. We have been dispersed. We have been separated along ethnic and linguistic lines. We have been tiny and weak in the face of a vast territory and a harsh climate. We have been immigrants and exiles.

As the executive director of CBC documentaries Mark Starowicz put it in his 2006 Symons Lecture in Charlottetown, "We are all boat people. We just got here at different times. The collective Canadian experience, however recent or buried in the ancestral past, is the memory of displacement and loss, followed by the collective experience of endurance and redemption."[3] Believe it or not, there is no meaningful *pure laine* in English Canada. (Quebec is another story, as we saw earlier in this book.) And if you worry that the people who were born in Canada and claim their ancestry as exclusively British might try to assert themselves as the real, true Canadians? Don't sweat it: even if they all agreed on this point and tried to form a movement, according to Statistics Canada they make up only 15 percent of the Canadian population.[4]

The days of this group running Canada are over. The exclusive private clubs some of them belong to need not lock the gates at night: no one else wants to get in.

The original working title of this book was *The Paradox of Canadian Chauvinism.* I see the paradox of our chauvinism as the idea that Canada is the greatest country in the world precisely because we don't think we're the greatest country in the world. Pessimism and anxiety are part of the national character (perhaps the results of displacement and loss Mark Starowicz speaks about). It takes courage in this country to say something positive, to flirt with optimism, because such thinking runs counter to the psyche of a risk-averse people who use pessimism as a defence mechanism against the fear of failure and ridicule, of making a mistake or being teased for naive optimism and idealism. Optimism and idealism are for Americans, not Canadians. We are a skeptical people, suspicious of anyone trying to sell us something. Americans reach for the stars and land a man on the moon. We predict disaster so that we can be relieved when it occasionally doesn't happen.

I expect that many will find my arguments in this book too optimistic. I can't change the national psyche any more than I can change the fact that this optimism I express about multicultural Canada comes from a white guy born at the right time in a small town in rural Canada who lives in a leafy neighbourhood in downtown Toronto. I can only hope that others will agree that my optimism is rooted in an honest examination of the data and a fair reading of our history as a people. We've come a long way in understanding and accommodating the other. Indeed, many Canadians have adopted curiosity about the other as part of their personal identity: in our values research, people tell us again and again that they think of themselves as people who try to learn from those who are different. They may not always succeed, they may fail to understand, they may even inadvertently offend. But to express the aspiration is a remarkable first step in a world where chauvinism and tribalism so often have the first word and the last.

Maybe one day we'll all come to see ourselves as minorities of one. And instead of feeling terrified we'll find ourselves capable of revelling in that solitude. Instead of two solitudes we'll have become thirty-two million. And after we're done narcissistically contemplating our own unique stew of mixed and melted identities, we'll head outside onto a Canadian street and see who else we can see.

Appendix
Environics Survey of Canadian Muslims

Environics surveyed five hundred adult Canadian Muslims between 30 November 2006 and 5 January 2007. The sample frame for this survey consisted of households in the ten provinces of Canada located within Census Canada dissemination areas (DAs) identified from current census data as having a high representation of people reporting their religious affiliation as Muslim. The sample was derived from telephone numbers assigned within the boundaries of these selected DAs. Quotas were used to allocate interviews by region in order to ensure representation from all regions. The final sample was then weighted by age, gender, and region based on population data. Comparisons of the sample from this survey and census data confirm that the Environics sample of Canadian Muslims was representative of the Canadian Muslim population at large.

The exact wording of the survey items discussed in chapter three follows.

SELECTED QUESTIONS

3. Would you say you are very, somewhat, not very, or not at all PROUD to be Canadian?

4. What is it about Canada that gives you the greatest sense of pride?

5. And what do you like least about Canada?

11. In your opinion, how many Canadians do you think are hostile toward Muslims? Would you say most, many, just some, or very few?

12. In the last two years, have you personally had a bad experience due to your race, ethnicity, or religion, or hasn't this happened to you?

15. [women only] Do you wear a hijab, niqab, or chador in public?

16. [women only] Over the past 30 days, how often have you worn a [hijab/niqab/chador] in public?

17. Some countries have decided to ban the wearing of head scarves by Muslim women in public places, including schools. Do you think this is a good idea or a bad idea?

20. Please tell me how worried you are about each of the following issues related to Muslims living in Canada. Are you very worried, somewhat worried, not too worried, or not at all worried?

   a. A decline in the importance of religion among Canada's Muslims

b. Muslim women in Canada taking on modern roles in society

c. The influence of music, movies, and television on Muslim youth in Canada

d. Unemployment among Canadian Muslims

e. Extremism among Canadian Muslims

f. Discrimination against Muslims

21. Do you think most Muslims coming to our country today want to adopt Canadian customs and way of life or do you think that they want to be distinct from the larger Canadian society?

29. To what extent do you feel that ordinary, law-abiding Muslim Canadians have a responsibility to report on potentially violent extremists they might encounter in their mosques and communities. Do they have a great deal of responsibility, some responsibility, or no responsibility at all for reporting on such activity?

30. Have you heard about the arrests of 18 Muslim boys and men in the Greater Toronto Area earlier this year, who were accused of plotting terrorist attacks on Canadian targets?

31. If these attacks had been carried out, do you think they would have been completely justified, somewhat justified, or not at all justified?

32. Whether or not you think the attacks were justified, do you personally have any sympathy with the feelings and motives of those who allegedly wanted to carry them out?

Notes

INTRODUCTION: THE GOOD NEWS AND THE BAD NEWS

1. Grant Schellenberg and Hélène Maheux, "Immigrants' Perspectives on Their First Four Years in Canada: Highlights from Three Waves of the Longitudinal Survey of Immigrants to Canada," Statistics Canada, 30 April 2007.

2. James S. Woodsworth, *Strangers Within Our Gates; or, Coming Canadians* (Toronto: University of Toronto Press, 1974).

1: IMMIGRATION, MULTICULTURALISM, AND CANADIAN IDENTITY

1. Pew Global Attitudes Project, "American Character Gets Mixed Reviews," 23 June 2005.

2. GlobeScan, "Israel and Iran Share Most Negative Ratings in Global Poll," 6 March 2007.

3. Philip Johnston, "Adopt Our Values or Stay Away, Says Blair," *Telegraph,* 10 December 2006.

4. "The Uncomfortable Politics of Identity," *The Economist,* 16 October 2006.

5. Craig Smith, "Anger Expected in Suburbs If Sarkozy Wins French Election," *International Herald-Tribune,* 4 May 2007.

6. Will Kymlicka, "Canadian Multiculturalism in Historical and Comparative Perspective: Is Canada Unique?" *Constitutional Forum,* 13.1 (2003): 1–8.

7. "The Failure of Multiculturalism," *National Post,* 25 August 2006.

8. Pierre Elliott Trudeau, "Announcement of Implementation of Policy of Multiculturalism within Bilingual Framework," House of Commons, Ottawa, 8 October 1971.

9. "International Social Trends Monitor," Ipsos MORI, May 2006. (Approximately one thousand interviews were conducted in each country.)

10. Unless otherwise noted, polling data are drawn from Focus Canada, Environics' quarterly omnibus survey which polls a random sample of two thousand Canadians.

11. "International Social Trends Monitor," Ipsos MORI, May 2006.

12. "Migration in an Interconnected World: New Directions for Action," Report of the Global Commission on International Migration, 2005.

13. "Multiculturalism, R.I.P. (1982–2007)," *National Post,* 24 April 2007.

14. Kymlicka, "Canadian Multiculturalism in Historical and Comparative Perspective," 1–8.

15. Allan Gregg, "Identity Crisis," *The Walrus,* March 2006.

16. Andrew Cohen, *The Unfinished Canadian* (Toronto: McClelland & Stewart, 2007).

17. Gad Horowitz, "Mosaics and Identity," in Bryan Finnigan and Cy Gonick, eds., *Making It: The Canadian Dream* (Toronto: McClelland & Stewart, 1972), 465–73.

18. David Ley, "Multiculturalism: A Canadian Defence," *Research on Immigration and Integration in the Metropolis. Working Paper Series,* 7.4, March 2007.

19. Environics Focus Canada, 2006.

2: THE FACTS ON THE GROUND

1. Feng Hou and Garnett Picot, "Visible Minority Neighbourhoods in Toronto, Montreal, and Vancouver," *Canadian Social Trends,* Statistics Canada, Spring 2004, Cat. 11-008.

2. Marina Jiménez, "Do Ethnic Enclaves Impede Integration?" *The Globe and Mail,* 8 February 2007.

3. Ley, "Muliticulturalism," 14.

4. Researchers define ghettos and enclaves in various ways, but generally a ghetto is understood to combine extreme ethnic concentration with isolation (and sometimes poverty), while an enclave is an area of ethnic concentration but not necessarily accompanied by isolation or poverty.

5. Although this area would not fall under the Statistics Canada definition of a visible minority enclave.

6. Nicholas Keung, "Ethnic Mini-Cities on Rise: StatsCan," *Toronto Star,* 10 March 2004.

7. Mohammad Qadeer and Sandeep Kumar, "Toronto's Ethnic Enclaves: Sites of Segregation or Communities of Choice?" CERIS Seminar Presentation, 19 May 2005, http://ceris.metro polis.net/events/seminars/2005/May/Sandeep1.pdf.

8. Feng Hou, "Recent Immigration and the Formation of Visible Minority Neighbourhoods in Canada's Large Cities" (Ottawa: Statistics Canada Analytical Studies Research Paper Series), Cat. 11F0019MIE-221.

9. Will Kymlicka, *Finding Our Way: Rethinking Ethnocultural Relations in Canada* (Toronto: Oxford University Press, 1998), 55.

10. Alan R. Walks and Larry S. Bourne, "Ghettos in Canada's Cities? Racial Segregation, Ethnic Enclaves and Poverty Concentration in Canadian Urban Areas," *The Canadian Geographer*, 50.3 (Fall 2006): 273–97.

11. Walter Benn Michaels, *The Trouble with Diversity* (New York: Metropolitan, 2006).

12. Schellenberg and Maheux, "Immigrants' Perspectives on Their First Four Years in Canada."

13. Garnett Picot, Feng Hou, and Simon Coulombe, "Chronic Low Income and Low-Income Dynamics Among Recent Immigrants" (Ottawa: Statistics Canada Analytical Studies Research Paper Series), Cat. 11F0019MIE2007294-294.

14. Jeffrey G. Reitz and Rupa Banerjee, "Racial Inequality, Social Cohesion, and Policy Issues in Canada," *Belonging? Diversity, Recognition and Shared Citizenship in Canada*, Keith Banting, Thomas J. Courchene, and F. Leslie Seidle, eds. (Montreal: Institute for Research on Public Policy, 2007), 489–545.

15. Peter S. Li, "Initial Earnings and Catch-up Capacity of Immigrants," *Canadian Public Policy*, 29.3, 2003.

16. Abdurrahman Aydemir, Wen-Hao Chen, and Miles Corak, "Intergenerational Earnings Mobility Among the Children of Canadian Immigrants" (Ottawa: Statistics Canada, Analytical Studies Branch Research Paper Series), Cat. 11F0019, No. 267, 25 October 2005.

17. *Ethnicity* in this discussion refers to self-identified ethnic origin on the census, and to single responses only. In the case of the riding of Vaughan, 55.6 percent of all residents describe themselves as only Italian—not of any mixed or hyphenated background.

18. Of course, there are plenty of ridings throughout the country where Canadian-born MPs were voted in by a group of electors whose ethnocultural background (British or French) almost universally matches their own—but we're dealing here with the question of whether foreign-born MPs are able to gain access to Parliament only if they're elected by "ghettos" or "enclaves" of their own people.

19. Anne Milan and Brian Hamm, "Mixed Unions," *Canadian Social Trends* (Ottawa: Statistics Canada), Summer 2004, Cat. 11-008.

3: MUSLIMS IN CANADA

1. Licia Corbella, "Disturbing Reality Buried," *Calgary Sun,* 18 February 2007.

2. Focus Canada, 2006.

3. Environics Social Values survey, 2005.

4. Ekos Research Associates, 2006. This research was conducted for the Public Health Agency of Canada's "HIV/AIDS Attitudinal Tracking Survey 2006," www.phac-aspc.gc.ca/aids-sida/publication/por/2006/51stigma_e.html.

5. Doug Saunders, "Why the Fear of a 'Muslim Tide' Makes Too Much of a Splash," *The Globe and Mail,* 14 April 2007.

4: QUEBEC: THE DISTINCT, DIVERSE SOCIETY

1. Tu Thanh Ha, "Straight Shooter Looks to Lead," *The Globe and Mail,* 6 September 2006.

2. From Focus Canada, 2006, volume 4. Note: This Canada-wide finding may seem to contradict some of the openness to immigration I described in chapter one. It's true: although large majorities of Canadians believe that immigrants make positive

contributions to the country, most Canadians also worry that too many immigrants aren't adopting Canadian values. I believe this impression is in large part a product of exactly the pessimism (propagated by public discourse that often fails to distinguish between the situation in Canada and the situations in other countries with large immigrant populations) that I'm attempting to address in this book.

3. In this measurement we defined WASP as white, Protestant, and claiming as their ethnic origin either British or Canadian.

CONCLUSION: WORKING ON UTOPIA

1. Melanie Phillips, "The Country That Hates Itself," *National Post*, 16 June 2006.

2. Kymlicka, *Finding Our Way*, 65.

3. Mark Starowicz, "Whose Story? Storytelling as Nationbuilding," Symons Lecture, Charlottetown, 8 November 2006.

4. Five percent of Canadians claim English as their sole ethnic heritage, and an additional 15 percent claim English as one of multiple ancestries.

Acknowledgments

This optimistic take on Canada's magnificent experiment with multiculturalism would not have been possible without the collaboration of my brilliant and remarkably composed colleague Amy Langstaff, who has worked with me on three of my previous publications and over time become a partner in this poll-driven book-creation enterprise. It is a partnership through which I think we have each learned much about Canadians' values, including our own.

As usual, Amy and I have been aided, abetted, and encouraged by a host of others. First, of course, is the team at Environics, led by its president Barry Watson. My assistant, Karen Thibault, coordinates significant swaths of my corporate life so as to free up some time for my imagination to work on writing projects, and for that I am deeply grateful. Time is a precious commodity for an author who has a day job.

We also drew upon the invaluable geodemographic analysis of our sister company, Environics Analytics, and wish to particularly thank Jan Kestle, the company's president; Delphic Doug Norris, senior vice president and chief demographer; and Rupen Seoni, vice president client services.

Another firm in the Environics family also played a unique role: Graham Loughton and his colleague Lisa Khan-Yee at Research House conducted the unprecedented survey of Canadian Muslims, the findings of which form the basis of chapter three of this book. Homaira Ghani, one of our frontline interviewers, emerged from the phone room to do a wonderful job discussing the interview process with the media. Overseeing this project was Environics Research senior vice president and quintessential researcher Keith Neuman, aided by senior associate and formidable information sponge Derek Leebosh. We owe thanks to all members of the team for executing to a very high standard this innovative and invaluable research.

Outside the Environics empire, we found plenty of generous support. Fellow research professional Kaan Yigit at Solutions Research Group and his colleague Ross Walton generously shared and discussed data from their pioneering multicultural research.

The magnificent people at Statistics Canada, under the leadership of Dr. Ivan Felegi, provided data from the census, the Ethnic Diversity Survey, and a number of other large and important surveys that were invaluable to us.

In the world of academe, we were privileged to spend incredibly helpful and inspiring time with one of Canada's, indeed one of the world's, great philosophers of multiculturalism, Will Kymlicka. We were also privileged to not only benefit from the work of but share thoughts in person with pre-eminent scholar Jeffrey Reitz and his impressive colleague Rupa Banerjee at the University of Toronto. Jack Jedwab, the executive director of the Association for Canadian Studies in Montreal, was also a great help. We are indebted to many others, including my old Queen's political science classmate, the estimable Keith Banting, and his polymath colleague Tom Courchene, who edited a valuable book on multiculturalism sponsored by the Institute for Research on Public Policy.

In this book and in others, when it has come to Canada's distinct society, Quebec, I have relied on insights from some native sons, including my friend and colleague Alain Giguère, president of the Quebec polling firm CROP. In addition, Jean Paré, former editor of *L'actualité,* generously interrupted a retirement schedule busier than most people's careers to share valuable insights on social change in Quebec.

I am also delighted to acknowledge my indebtedness to two people I admire, one a courageous publisher and the other a respected professional colleague. Ken Alexander, the founder, editor in chief, and champion of *The Walrus,* English Canada's pre-eminent magazine of ideas, published an insightful and provocative article on multiculturalism by my fellow pollster Allan Gregg in the spring of 2006. I was first inspired to respond to Allan's essay in the pages of *The Walrus,* but soon found my response to be rather too lengthy for even that magazine's capacious pages. So to Ken and Allan, thank you for the inspiration to take on this book project.

Finally, of course, I must thank my literary agent, Bruce Westwood, who is always ready with a glass of Prosecco to soothe an anxious author; my serene and brilliant publisher, David Davidar; and my diplomatic yet persuasive editor, Diane Turbide, who is always able to inspire me to do better.

To these folks and those many thousands of Canadians who answer our questions at all hours of the day and night, and especially the five hundred Muslim Canadians for whom answering our survey was perhaps yet another adventure in Canadian citizenship, we owe our very deepest thanks and respect.

Index

Italicized numerals refer to charts, graphs, notes.